Organizational Intelligence

How smart companies use information to
become more **competitive** and **profitable**

BY GERALD COHEN
AND RADO KOTOROV, Ph.D.

ISBN: 978-0-692-76959-1

Printed in the U.S.A. September 2016

Contents

"The degree of organizational intelligence within an enterprise is directly proportional to the level of information distribution to its stakeholders. The more people get quality information for decision-making, the more fact-based decisions they will make, and the more standard the decision process in the organization will be. Even though there is no exact measure today for organizational intelligence, we believe that measuring the pervasiveness of information distribution can provide a solid foundation for the development of such a measure."

Gerry Cohen

"In today's hyper-competitive market, companies have to be agile, smart, and fast. Organizational intelligence is the only foundation upon which these three capabilities can be built."

Rado Kotorov, Ph.D.

Preface

Since the invention of computers, organizations worldwide have continuously made investments to capture and process more and more data in order to improve their decision-making and overall efficiency. Today this field is known as *business intelligence and analytics*. The goal of business intelligence and analytics has been to empower more fact-based decision-making, as opposed to decisions based on intuition and partial information. The overall improvement of the decision-making process through information dissemination leads to higher organizational intelligence and market performance.

At Information Builders, we also believe that it is equally important to empower not just the management team, but every employee in the organization with access to information to make fact-based decisions on the job. It is an interesting coincidence that shortly after Information Builders was founded, a Nobel Prize was awarded for studies in decision-making. In his 1978 acceptance speech for the Nobel Prize, Herbert Simon stated, "In the study of organizations, the employee must be the focus of attention, for the success of the structure will be judged by his performance within it." He emphasized, "The behavior of individuals is the tool with which the organization achieves its targets." [1] The goal to empower every employee with information still remains aspirational, as BI and analytics have only about 22% penetration in organizations. The 78% of employees who do not get access to information are typically operational employees. Profits are made and costs are incurred in operations. Hence, leaving these employees out of the enterprise BI and analytics system makes performance less than optimal. Since the organizational performance directly correlates with the degree of information dissemination to all employees and stakeholders, we hope that the approaches and the examples in this book will help organizations grow the adoption of BI and analytics beyond the 22%. [2]

We decided to start this book with a review of our history at Information Builders, starting in 1975, and how we changed as the technology around us changed, and what we learned from this experience. The stable part of our story is the continuing need for information by our customers and their employees to be able to run their organizations. Having a stable marketplace is a great advantage, especially when so many new products today seem to service transient needs.

We live in times when the technology changes very fast, and when new technologies are introduced with great hype. This makes it difficult for enterprises to decide which technologies to adopt and how to discern value from fad. There is a high percentage of what we call *flare and glare technologies* that waste time and other organizational resources prior to disappearing from the market. Making decisions about new technologies is not easy, because there are no facts, and no data has been collected on their usage and value. In the absence of such data and prior experience, the only way to make decisions is by using historical analogies. Let me give you an example.

When mobile devices started to be deployed in the enterprise, there was a strong push to develop native applications for the BlackBerry® device. User experience advocates were adamant about the benefits of such BI and analytics applications. They ignored the high costs of building mobile applications for the BlackBerry. We estimated that BI for the BlackBerry would cost approximately one-third of the entire enterprise BI cost. There were small start-ups that created sample applications that drove the hype. So everyone was pushing us to jump on the bandwagon and build such an app. We were concerned that the cost would inhibit adoption, but we could not ignore the noise in the market. Damned if you do, damned if you don't. So how do you decide what approach to take?

We looked at the history of applications and the movement from the desktop to the browser. Since the browser was the most common denominator for information delivery and the cheapest way to distribute informational applications, we decided in 1995 to focus on browser-based delivery of BI and analytics, and applied the same approach to our mobile solutions.

We hope that the historical perspective will help you navigate today's technology landscape and discern value from hype when investing in emerging technologies and trends. We also hope that it will illustrate the key fact that guided our technology choices: the demand for information has been steadily increasing over time. We have observed that companies that disseminate information to satisfy this demand at all levels of the organization have become more competitive and attracted more customers. We can infer that there is a direct correlation between information dissemination and organizational performance. Even in uncertain times when the technologies change rapidly, investing in technologies that raise your organizational intelligence by disseminating information to more users is a safe bet.

Part One

Organizational Intelligence:
Technology Evolution, Proliferation,
and User Diversification

Introduction

Every new technology is initially developed to solve simple needs. But, as it evolves, it extends to satisfy more diverse and deeper needs. The technology also becomes more complex. The users start to stratify themselves based on their needs and their skills. In turn, this drives the evolution of new tools that are more tailored to particular needs and skills. In parallel, new approaches and strategies are being developed to drive the adoption of these technologies among diverse stakeholders. This book describes this dynamic and makes recommendations on how to build an overall strategy for organizational intelligence, and how to tailor the approach to different constituencies in order to maximize adoption and value.

Chapter 1: The Beginning of Business Intelligence: Making Data Querying Easy	Discusses how we formed Information Builders to satisfy a simple, basic need.
Chapter 2: The Influence of Technology on Business Intelligence	Discusses the emergence and evolution of different technologies and their impact on business intelligence (BI).
Chapter 3: The Origin of the Informational Application	Discusses the difference between self-service and pervasive information distribution for decision-making.
Chapter 4: Different Users, Different Needs	Discusses the different user types, their skills, their needs, and their decision-making styles.
Chapter 5: Building Pervasive Organizational Intelligence	Discusses why organizations need to develop pervasive organizational intelligence systems.
Chapter 6: Data Monetization and Informational Applications	Discusses how data is quickly becoming the most important strategic asset in organizations and why data monetization should be made part of every business model.
Chapter 7: Summary of Business Drivers for Different Types of InfoApps	Provides a summary of the key business drivers and benefits for each of the types of InfoApps within our taxonomy of organizational intelligence.

Chapter One

The Beginning of Business Intelligence:
Making Data Querying Easy

The World's Most Successful Apps

I think it is safe to say that the Apple® iPad® probably contains more computer applications than any other device in the world. These apps are always easy to use, or at least do not require a user manual, so that they can provide their intended service with no training. In many cases, the intent of the app is to provide information to the user. For example, the weather app helps users check weather conditions in any city, and the airline apps allow users to check flight status, stand-by information, upgrades, etc. These types of informational applications, where the user interacts with data, are the subject of this book.

A long history of technological invention has been necessary to reach today's level of capability with the level of simplicity that makes these apps so popular. Forty years ago, the software industry was a world without fonts; charting and display capabilities were primitive and mono-color, and yet as I will describe, it had the basics for what today we call business intelligence.

In broad terms, business intelligence originated as a set of technologies and methodologies to provide business users with information to make better decisions. As the volumes of data grew, business intelligence started to attract more and more users, and naturally needed to adapt the tools and information delivery methods to professionals with different needs and skill levels. This diversification of the user base

Today, Business Intelligence is increasingly being used to provide information to partners, suppliers, and customers – a rapidly evolving field known as customer-facing apps.

occurs naturally in maturing industries. Consider, for example, the wide proliferation of different types of computers. Gamers need powerful configurations and monitors; road warriors need less power, but more compact machines; and many casual users are happy with just a tablet and a marketplace to get the simple-to-use apps that they need. Today, business intelligence is increasingly being used to provide information to partners, suppliers, and customers – a rapidly evolving field known as customer-facing apps.

Because of the wide diversification of user needs and technologies, we consider it more appropriate to talk about organizational intelligence. This term encompasses all information-related technologies, such as business intelligence, advanced analytics, decision support, etc. It more accurately captures the desire that today's organizations have to raise their overall organizational intelligence by providing more information to all stakeholders to support fact-based decision-making.

I am going to take you back a good many years to describe my perspective of how and what drove the evolution of the technology to its state today, and also what we learned from this early experience. I will also describe how we started by making self-service data querying easy, and how we ended up in the business of organizational business intelligence and pervasive distribution of information.

The Emergence of Direct User/Computer Interaction

I started Information Builders together with two partners in 1975 to solve a bottleneck problem. All of the information an organization had was locked up in the tapes and small disk drives in the computer center, and there was no easy way to unlock this information and use it to solve business problems on a daily basis. At that time, almost all computers used punch cards to enter input. Upon completion of the computer job, a printout of the result was available. There was no interaction between the user and the computer.

I was fortunate that one of the new IBM® 360 computers was available to me. It was the model 67 and used the time-sharing operating system called CP/CMS.[3] Time-sharing was a new type of operating system and allowed multiple people to use a computer simultaneously. Think of it as a ring, where each person gets a small slice of computer power as the computer goes around the ring of users. The other innovation was the use of Teletype-like terminals to enter data remotely via the telephone. We were about to enter a new era of computing without punch cards.

Time-sharing started a new industry of *service bureaus,* for example, Unisys®, General Electric®, Tymshare, and National CSS. They offered *time-sharing* computing services.[4] Users could send data or type in data to the service bureau, and then via a terminal, get information, run an application, and perform all of the functions that an in-house computer could do. If this sounds familiar when compared with today's cloud computing, you are correct. But that is another story.

Users had two-way access to their data on the computer via their Teletype-like keyboard. The speed was a little better than three characters per second, but increased quickly in a short time. Even though the Teletype keyboard held the promise of replacing the punch cards, one other invention was necessary for all the service bureau customers to connect to the computer in the first place.

In 1968, the Federal Communications Commission (FCC) allowed devices not sanctioned by AT&T, such as the Carterfone, to be connected directly to the AT&T network, as long as they did not cause harm to the system. The Carterfone ruling (13 F.C.C.2d 420) opened the possibilities for creating other devices that could connect to the phone system, and opened the market to customer-owned equipment. The decision opened the way for later innovations, including answering machines, fax machines, and modems. Manufacturers soon started to turn out faster terminals with soft-eared modems that attached to the telephone. AT&T soon joined the bandwagon, and provided simpler connections to a telephone, and faster speeds. The inter-connectedness of the world was off and running.[5]

By 1977, we had CRT terminals supplementing the typewriter-like terminals.[6] On a CRT terminal, both the output from the computer, and the input from the user, appeared interlaced as the dialogue continued. Now people could interact directly with a computer in a question/answer type of session. This had the extra benefit of reducing the use of paper, thus saving a lot of trees.

The main problem though was not speed or the hardware limitations, but the nature of the person-to-computer interaction. The only way to get information out of any database was to write a common business-oriented language (COBOL) program. COBOL was designed in 1959 specifically for data processing. Its only data types were numbers and strings of text. It was widely adopted, not because it was easy to use, but in part because the Department of Defense required computer manufacturers to adopt it.[7] Even though it was intended to have an English-like syntax to help facilitate adoption, its language became verbose and convoluted to some, making it difficult to learn. It became the province of the programmer.

Ordinary users did not pick up on the COBOL language. I even recall a scientific debate about whether some people without mathematical skills had the aptitude for learning programming.[8] In computer programming, whenever something is difficult to learn and perform, it is often attributed to lack of aptitude rather than poor design. However, there is no evidence that mathematical aptitude is required for learning programming. It was clear that there was opportunity to create a query language for non-technical people. I should also mention that all of this was occurring before the emergence of relational databases and Structured Query Language (SQL).

A Self-Service Query Language

We started to experiment using English as a natural language to talk to a database. We believed that the more the computer language resembled the mother tongue of the users, the easier it would be to learn. So, we came up with a structured English language with a simple syntax that was easy to remember and use. For example, the phrase SUM SALES would do exactly that: sum up the data fields named SALES. The phrase SUM SALES BY PRODUCT IF THE YEAR IS 1975 would create a row for each PRODUCT with SALES in the next column, all filtered for the YEAR 1975. One of the

Modem[9]

CRT terminal[10]

The main problem though was not speed or the hardware limitations, but the nature of the person-to-computer interaction. The only way to get information out of any database was to write a COBOL (common business-oriented language) program.

reasons why it is hard to learn programming languages is that the words do not have natural meanings, making them hard to remember. We solved exactly this problem.

We called this the **FOCUS** language, a mnemonic for **F**or **O**nline **C**omputer **U**ser**S**, and we eventually filled all of the language constructions that were needed to get answers to business questions from databases. For example, the business analysts might want a report with a subtotal when the PRODUCT changes, or a SUBFOOT, or SUBHEAD, which are in the domain of report formatting. So we expanded the syntax to provide such options, but kept it understandable and easy to use. This provided the logical foundation for the simple end-user query language.

Now we could *talk* to the data, but we also needed to construct a standard way to describe the data and the type of data fields, because each of the current databases had a different way of doing this. We had to construct a metadata layer to describe the data in the database. The metadata layer helps the user to understand the underlying data structure without having to know the particulars of each database. Think of it as a voice-directed GPS navigation versus reading a physical map. For many people, learning the symbols on a map and relating them to the physical environment is difficult. Voice navigation makes it simple to go where you want, without learning cartography. Similarly, metadata provided English-like descriptions for the database constructs, making it easier for users to understand and remember.

Metadata described the names of the *fields*, the type of data, such as numbers or letters, and if it was a number, which computer format it was in, such as integer or floating point decimal places. We came up with a very simple syntax for this, and it was inclusive enough to fit all of the then prevalent databases, including VSAM, IMS, and comma-separated. This syntax has been expanded over the years to cover all of the new kinds of data, such as geographical data, and today's NoSQL big data.

We even invented our own database, the FOCUS database, because it was important for users to see not only aggregates and details, but also the breakdown by categories. Most business organizations are hierarchically structured. The people at the top want to see the whole picture, as well as a breakdown of the results for their divisions or managers. Hence, there was a natural demand for putting a structure around the data that could represent the business organization and fulfill each manager's particular need for information. The FOCUS database design was hierarchical; it organized the data by segmenting it and nesting lower segments into higher segments. For example, in a hierarchical database, a segment for PRODUCT_PACKAGE could contain data at the lowest level of granularity – the package size, price, etc. Since it is at the lowest level, it could be nested in the higher segment PRODUCT_NAME, which in turn could be nested in the higher segment for PRODUCT_CATEGORY. Each segment contains its detail fields and the whole hierarchy can be JOINed or MATCHed to other fields across structures.

Today, some people refer to a MATCH as a BLEND because it can work after aggregation. In other words, the analyst can run two separate queries against two different data structures, where one returns sales results for states and counties, and the other returns local advertising costs for each county. The analyst may want to put the results in one report in order to see whether local advertising costs correlate with sales. To do this, the analysts will MATCH or BLEND the results of the two queries by relating the two files based on the county field. Thus, where the counties are the same, sales and cost can be seen together and a calculation can be made, such as calculating advertising as a percent of sales.

The result of all this work was a simple query language to explore data for our users and break it down by any level in the organization – the product catalog, geography, and so on.

The first version of FOCUS was offered on the Tymshare service bureau at the end of 1975. We prepared a card for the sales people with ten talking points for them to remember when speaking with a prospect. The first point was *Easy-to-use English query language*. I confess that I cannot find a single copy of this card after 40 years, and I only remember one other point, which was *See your data in a graph*. We were able to create bar charts using text characters to visualize each bar, and we created line charts by using dots. Now we were poised to deal with real-life customers.

When I tried to summarize what we learned from this experience, it occurred to me that in business, the biggest lesson is always synthesized in a short sentence that is promptly displayed on sales materials. In our case, as I noted previously, this was *Easy-to-use English query language.* This became the value proposition for the customer, but it was not the whole story.

Meet the Customer

The service was launched at the end of 1975, and went full blast in 1976. I remember very clearly speaking to our sponsor, and was surprised at his reaction when I told him that we had attained our first customer. He reminded me that there is a huge difference between zero and one, that is, getting to the point of having your first customer. I must say that I never forgot this, and have used this analogy on many occasions, especially when launching new products. The inventor of PayPal® even wrote a book on the difference between zero and one (*Zero to One,* by Peter Thiel with Blake Masters), so I guess every generation of entrepreneurs has to learn this important concept.

Tymshare had modified the CP/CMS operating system to their own specifications, and had also invented an early mini-computer that could concentrate telephone traffic at large customer centers and control their connection to the service bureau computers. Needless to say, they were very successful in signing up new customers for this new capability. Because they offered a worldwide service, large companies could consolidate their data and see how they were doing across all of their divisions and locations. It was then that enterprise-level decision support, business intelligence, or business analytics was born.[11]

Today there is still some debate about the difference among those three terms, but most people use them interchangeably. The definitional differences are somewhat artificial, because all of them describe the use of information for decision-making. Business intelligence has become the most widely used term.

The variety of applications spanned every industry. We were swamped with adding new features, handling new databases, and most interestingly, working with the users of our software.

Pervasiveness has become the primary goal of BI, and the ultimate criteria for success, as it enables organizations to establish fact-based decision-making at any level of the organization.

Surviving Our First Market Disruption

Many future technological disruptions were going to occur. But the first was perhaps the most instructive. This was in 1979, with the introduction of low-priced computers that were capable of running a time-sharing operating system. Most important to us was the IBM 4300 series of computers. This meant that our service bureau customers could convert to their own in-house computers. This was not only a life-and-death struggle for Tymshare and all of the products sold on their network, it was also the first major disruption that we survived. Since then, we have been surviving industry disruptions for more than 40 years. Here is how it happened.

We had the foresight at the time to start to build a sales force of our own and began selling FOCUS to in-house customers. By 1985, Tymshare went out of business, as did the whole time-sharing industry eventually. Suddenly, we found ourselves becoming a software company, selling a product to customers who needed to distribute information to all of the people in their organization who made decisions, namely everyone. In ten years, we graduated from the do-it-yourself school of products to a different level of pervasive information distribution.

Since then, pervasiveness has become the primary goal of BI and the ultimate criteria for success, as it enables organizations to establish fact-based decision-making at any level of the organization. Most importantly, it distributes information not just to executives, but also to operational workers whose decisions and actions have direct impact on the bottom line. Pervasiveness also means extending information distribution to partners and suppliers, to align their performance with the organizational strategy in order to achieve higher efficiency levels. Finally, pervasiveness means delivering information to the customer and receiving a greater share of wallet, higher lifetime value, and lower attrition rates.

And while pervasiveness has been an aspirational goal of the entire BI industry, it still remains elusive for many organizations today. As industry analyst Cindi Howson points out, despite all efforts for the last 25 years, BI has modest penetration of about 22% of enterprise users.[12] This book describes what we learned about how to deliver information to the masses and make BI pervasive. Because if there is one lesson to be learned from pervasive information distribution, it is that information distribution changes the organizational behavior and drives performance to new levels. In turn, this results in lower costs and higher revenues. Today we call this data monetization, or using data to derive more value from all resources, processes, stakeholders, and customers.

Chapter Two

The Influence of Technology on Business Intelligence (1978-2015)

Solving the Information Access Challenge

Technology determines what can be done and the rest is up to the ingenuity of people to use it for beneficial purposes. Before we even started to work on FOCUS, one totally unexpected event had to happen. This was the 1956 AT&T consent decree with the U.S. Government. Up until this time, all traffic that passed through a telephone was controlled by AT&T. But by 1956, it became obvious that this was limiting the possibilities of what could be done, such as translating tones into characters that could be visible on an appropriate device.

Also in 1956, scientists from Bell Labs were awarded a Nobel Prize for inventing transistors, which were noted as the "building blocks of integrated circuits and microchips." The invention of the transistor was a monumental technology development. As part of the 1956 AT&T consent decree, AT&T was required to release the transistor patent to the public, removing any opportunity for them to earn royalties from other companies' development of transistor technology. Since the opportunities for transistor technology development went far beyond the phone signal application, and perhaps to show compliance with the consent decree, AT&T offered to share the technology for a price of $25,000. Some companies who accepted the offer made the most of that investment, for example, General Electric, Texas Instruments, IBM.[13]

Technology determines what can be done and the rest is up to the ingenuity of people to use it for beneficial purposes.

The time from 1960, when computers started to be adopted on a large scale for data processing, to 1975 was dominated by COBOL programming for data processing. This was extremely expensive, and the industry was in a constant search for less costly and more easy-to-use technologies, as explained in Chapter 1, thus creating the opportunity to develop FOCUS.

AT&T's modem from 1958[14]

However, from our start, we went through some dramatic advances that also benefited our effort to connect our customers with their data. Here is a short recital of the technology advances and what they meant for business intelligence. The first few years we were in business (1975-1980) were influenced mostly by technological improvements in the ability to communicate with computers and to get printed results. In 1979, the Epson® MX 80 printer was the first easy-to-use, fast, dot matrix printer. It was the breakthrough machine that set dot matrix printing on the way to take over printing for a decade. So with a rabbit ear modem and a dot matrix printer, a time-sharing user could get by successfully.

The chart of significant technology inventions and developments is shown in the following image.

	IBM Mainframe **1952**
Modem **1958**	IBM VM/CMS **1972**
Tymshare **1973**	Terminals and Scopes **1976**
Dot Matrix Printer **1979**	PC DOS **1982**
Client/Server Computing and Apple Macintosh **1984**	HTML and Java **1990**
JavaScript and Netscape **1994**	Windows 95 **1995**
Google **1996**	Wi-Fi **1999**
64-bit processor **2003**	iPhone **2007**
iPad **2010**	HTML5 **2014**

Technology influence timeline

The corresponding advances in the features we introduced over the years paralleled this list. For example, in 1965, IBM was considered to have 65% of the market share, with all other competitor companies sharing the remaining 35%. IBM was referred to as "Snow White," while the seven competing companies were known as "the Seven Dwarfs."[15] By 1982, it could be said that IBM's dominance of personal computing was being eroded. A 15-year era of distributed computing started, where companies moved computer operations closer to manufacturing plants. We didn't want to be left out of this market expansion, so we reorganized ourselves into divisions to serve the major mini-computer manufacturers. The primary one was Digital Equipment Corporation, but also Hewlett-Packard, Wang, Data General, Tandem, and others. This contributed two very important skills to our technical abilities.

The first was that we figured out how to partition our software so that it could be run on different hardware platforms without a lot of changes. In effect, we created something akin to a Java® Virtual Machine architecture, or an abstract computing machine. But our server was still in C, which is still the most efficient language for new machine architectures.

The second was that each vendor and machine had different databases, with widely different features. For example, DEC invented RDB, their proprietary SQL database. It competed with IBM DB2®, but had some unique features. The construction of the database business grew apace with the new machines. There was furious competition in the SQL world, with Oracle® emerging as a dominant database vendor.

But there were lots of non-SQL databases also. I remember that we had object-oriented databases, and then object relational databases. These seem to have disappeared. We had variations of IBM VSAM, which were highly indexed but essentially sequential databases. Our ability to read all of these gave us a clear edge when client-server computing arrived. In fact, we built a separate technology group that is still in place today, so that we can very quickly attach to any new data source.

It's been a long gap, but with the advent of new technology, today we are starting to see new types of databases again. The drivers would appear to be faster storage speeds, but I think in this case, the restrictions of SQL are the biggest driver. When multiple competing companies get together in a standards organization, such as ISO or ANSI, it's likely that change will be very slow. The advent of NoSQL (Not only SQL) is

…the adapters and the metadata shielded the end user from this complexity, making the adoption of BI and analytics technologies much more straightforward for the non-technical user and the business analyst.

a healthy incentive to the database world. So today we boast access to every NoSQL database, like MongoDB® and all the Apache Hadoop® data systems.

We also realized that it wasn't just the data that could keep us out, but also the application providers, like SAP®, PeopleSoft®, and Salesforce®, who we had to navigate through to get to the data. Hence, we developed adapters for applications too. In this way, end users had no barriers to access and analyze data in any data store and application. It is our philosophy that the end user should not be burdened with the technical details of the different data stores, the different data schemas, and different query languages. So, the adapters and the metadata shielded the end user from this complexity, making the adoption of BI and analytics technologies much more straightforward for the non-technical user and the business analyst.

The Emergence of the PC
When IBM introduced the PC in 1982, we were among the earliest to receive one. Imagine our surprise to find that it had a memory of only 64 kilobytes. So, we bought an external memory board and figured out how to treat the PC like all of the other machines we ran on. Another surprise was that each manufacturer had its own version of the operating system DOS. It took a few years for PC DOS, or really MS-DOS®, to finally take over. By then we were in the early client-server years. Fortunately we were able to connect PC users with all of the remote databases, and PC/FOCUS did quite well.

Although we were watching Apple and the evolution of the Apple Macintosh® and its unique features, it didn't influence our direction because it was considered a personal computer and didn't sit on many of our customers' desks.

But in 1995, we were all over the new Microsoft Windows® 95 release, which was the full GUI release in which application windows were introduced. This was a significant step up from the previous Microsoft Windows releases, 1.0 which featured fixed windows, and the innovative subsequent releases that made overlapping windows a reality. This meant that multiple applications could be run simultaneously and displayed side-by-side. But it also facilitated the development of dialog boxes that overlapped with the application windows, which simplified the user interactions with the operating system and the software programs.

In 1996, we visited Netscape® and saw our first Internet browser, and it was soon on many of our developers' desktops. For 20 years, we had been working with essentially a time-sharing paradigm. But in 1994, we started to create a new product, which we called WebFOCUS, the son of FOCUS. It started with tiled screens and the introduction of visual objects, some in GIF form, and others generated by us as charts, but it quickly evolved into a web-based platform with many browser-based tools. The migration from the desktop to the browser made it easier to provision those tools to a larger number of users.

Together with WebFOCUS, we needed to shift from a language to a graphical user interface (GUI). This was a long process, as our users were comfortable with creating their content through the FOCUS language. That is not only a separate story, but one that is continuing even today, as the fashions in tools are always evolving. For example, with the evolution of self-service for business users and analysts, as part of a business intelligence solution, we need to simplify how non-technical users can do complex things without having to learn a computer language. It is not that the problems they want to solve are complicated, but dealing with the intricacies of Information Technology (IT) has its intrinsic problems. So the paradigm has shifted from trying to simplify the computer language, as we did with FOCUS, to simplifying the user interactions with the systems through a GUI.

To make this simpler, we created a *metadata* layer in WebFOCUS that allowed the IT developer to categorize their data so that the less experienced user would have some hints about the structure of the data. The metadata layer allowed us to give business

The only lock-in a company should consider is in constant change and adaptation, that is, lock its strategy and implementation into flexible solutions that can be easily migrated from one technology to another.

names to the cryptic database naming conventions, as well to automate the generation of complex queries that would have confused the business user or caused errors in the report. Two such problems are fan and chasm traps, which do exactly that, trap the user into an error. Thus, another component of WebFOCUS was born – the metadata/semantic layer – and was continuously improved.

Proliferation of Different Databases

In the early 2000s, because of the explosion of data collection and strong demand for analytics, there was a flurry of products whose purpose was to organize data into logical structures. Supposedly, these were to make accessing data easier. None of these products survived, and I believe that the major reason for that is because the database industry wasn't about to standardize on anything. This is still a common phenomenon. Venders rarely implement the latest SQL standards from ISO and ANSI in the same way.

In the early 2000s, many Online Analytical Processing (OLAP) databases appeared. Their purpose was to shorten the time it took to answer a query. All had their own proprietary standards. The decline of these OLAP cube databases is a good lesson in how just the raw power of computing improvements can make current solutions obsolete. It was again largely driven by the desire to simplify the implementation of BI and analytics. OLAP cubes were notoriously difficult to build and maintain. New technologies, such as larger memory, faster chips, and new database designs, have replaced these OLAP systems with in-memory computing, column-oriented databases, and highly parallel processing (for example, Apache Hadoop). The lesson to be learned is that if a company wants to stay relevant with its BI and analytics, it has to adopt the new technology, but not put all of its chips on it. This requires a flexible architecture that is modular, so that you can easily transition from one database type to another, thus avoiding costly lock-ins.

This is relevant today with cloud adoption. We maintain that our customers should be able to move their BI assets freely from one cloud vendor to another, to take advantage of any cost reductions in cloud-based services. In other words, the only lock-in a company should consider is in constant change and adaptation, for example, lock its strategy and implementation into flexible solutions that can be easily migrated from one technology to another.

> The goal of business intelligence is fairly simple: to provide information to all the people who need it so they can make better and faster decisions.

The Emergence of Visualizations

Bringing our story up to today's industrial needs highlights the diversity that new technology is making possible. In the 1980s, all output from a computer was character-based and went to paper. This meant that the output would be a printed report or a simple chart. In the 1990s, output started to appear on higher resolution screens, then to pure digital screens. This in turn stimulated the production of charts and a mixture of content, reports, charts, pictures, onto dashboards and sophisticated documents (such as analytical booklets, brochures, newsletters, magazines, and annual reports), and finally onto devices of various sizes.

The evolution of visualization is quite an interesting phenomenon. It all started with the idea that a picture is worth a thousand words. Hence, simple charts for descriptive statistics, such as bar and pie charts, were the first addition to the BI suite of tools. But even this was not simple. Users needed low-resolution charts for the web and high-resolution charts for print. The resolution of the chart determines the file size. High-resolution charts take more time to be rendered on the web. On the other hand, low-resolution charts appear pixilated when printed. So we had to build a chart generation engine that produced both. That way, the user can choose the targeted output – print or web – and the charts can be properly generated.

Then Macromedia® invented Flash® and animations became popular on the web. Naturally people wanted animated charts, so we had to add the Flash output format for our charts. The animation started a whole new field of innovations – visual interactivity. The interactive visualizations allowed the users to manipulate the data and perform analysis directly on the dashboards. That created a whole new market segment in the BI and analytics space that is known today as data discovery.

Not only did we create data discovery capabilities, but we also detected early the emergence of the mobile device as a medium for BI delivery. Interestingly enough,

Apple banned Flash-based applications from their mobile devices; thus, a new technology had to be invented to deliver interactivity on the mobile device. This is when we added JavaScript charts to our output formats. We also invented Active Technologies for interactive data exploration. Active Technologies combine the data, layout of the documents, and the analytic engine into a single HTML file. Unlike with static PDFs, users can interact with the content. We call this in-document analytics, as users can analyze the contents of the document without leaving the document. In the past, they had to export this data to Excel® to analyze it. It is worth mentioning that this format was invented and patented before HTML5 emerged, which made web interactivity mainstream.

The Emergence of Mobile BI

The goal of business intelligence is fairly simple: to provide information to all the people who need it so they can make better and faster decisions. Well, if you have a smartphone, you qualify as a BI user. This adds a new set of requirements for the BI providers, to include every type of display device. It's interesting that some companies charge extra for mobile BI and the delivery of information to the small digital screens, but if you look at this as just the medium of delivering the information, mobile delivery is just another output. To use an analogy, movie producers do not make a distinction between theater screens, TVs, laptops, tablets, and phones. It is up to the user where to watch the movie. This is an important development, as the number of devices and databases are ever increasing, as are protocols for passing information, types of security systems, computing environments, and so on. We have to build the technology in a way that does not increase the cost to the end users as new devices emerge.

Today, users do not have to be sitting at their desks to access and analyze information. Users can be on mobile devices. Thus, business intelligence has also become portable and we had to adapt to this new need without raising the cost of implementation. The first serious mobile device for business was the BlackBerry. Today the BlackBerry is almost extinct, but at the time of its initial release, it was considered the ultimate symbol of a serious business executive who was constantly connected to work regardless of time or distance. Email was the key feature of the BlackBerry mobile device. We developed a technology where users could run a report from these mobile devices. Not just receive a report as an attachment, but users could actually

We developed very deep technology to allow our customers
to construct sophisticated applications for their non-technical
users, who are the vast majority in any organization.

send parameters to the server to get exactly the information that they needed. This
made the BlackBerry the first mobile device to which we sent a report.
Then came the iPhone® and the iPad®, which firmly established mobile BI and
analytics as a sub-segment. What was available on the desktop had to be made
available on the mobile devices too. This forced us to rethink our output formats, and
add some new capabilities to our development and analysis tools so that the users
could design content once and use it on any device. This was technologically
challenging, as the mobile browsers and screens had their own distinct functionality,
such as touch screens, gesture support, and menus suitable for finger tapping.

The Challenge Ahead

Throughout all these years, we had two basic constituencies: the non-technical user
and the business user. We developed very deep technology to allow our customers
to construct sophisticated applications for their non-technical users, who are the vast
majority in any organization. We also allowed business users to use our facilities to get
quick answers to their questions. The latest development in this area is a separate
edition of WebFOCUS just for business users. It has the ability to connect with the full
WebFOCUS system, so that the larger business information systems can be
constructed with entry points for self-service users to also use the data in these
production systems.

As you read in the next chapters, where our customers describe how they use BI in
their business, note how a taste of success increases the desire to do even more.
That's our challenge.

In the following chapters, we categorize the kinds of applications for which BI
applications can be used. Since it is estimated that only about 22%[16] of the people in
large organizations have access to BI software, there is a long way to go to fully farm
its benefits for non-technical people. A more strategic shift to organizational

intelligence will help to drive adoption of fact-based decision-making among the rank-and-file employees in the organization, as well as within the extended enterprise that includes suppliers, partners, and customers. In Part 2 of the book, we provide a series of stories from actual customers, in their words, that describe how they monetized their ideas in the applications they built.

Chapter Three

The Origin of the Informational Application

Self-Service vs. Pervasive Information Distribution

This is a book about the transition from self-service to large-scale pervasive information distribution. The term self-service gained popularity recently in BI and analytics, and denotes the ability of a user to access data and perform analysis independently, without any support from IT. In most cases, this user is a business analyst, who uses a tool such as WebFOCUS InfoAssist, Microsoft® Power BI, Tableau®, or Qlik® Sense, to access corporate data sources or personal data files and to perform various types of analyses.

Yet, the vast majority of users do not want to learn any tools or configure access to any data sources, nor drag and drop fields to build reports or visualizations. They simply want to get factual answers to the questions they have. This field of providing information in an easily consumable way to non-technical users is called *pervasive information distribution*. It can take many different forms and user interfaces, but essentially it makes getting answers from data as easy as booking a flight online with Expedia.com®.

The key point that needs to be understood is that self-service tools have a natural limit. Ultimately they either become a constraint for the adoption of BI and analytics, or self-service is transformed into information distribution, that is, servicing the information needs of other non-technical and non-mathematically oriented

> ... the vast majority of users do not want to learn any tools or configure access to any data sources, nor drag and drop fields to build reports or visualizations. They simply want to get factual answers to the questions they have.

employees who need information to make decisions. The natural limit may be the skills required to learn to use a tool or the time required to make decisions. In either case, this requires a different approach to providing information to such decision-makers.

Understanding the difference between self-service and pervasive information distribution is important, as it helps enterprise leaders plan a BI and analytics strategy that maximizes the adoption among all stakeholders.

We are telling the story about the evolution from self-service to information distribution from a historical perspective to illustrate an important lesson – as the demand for information for decision-making grows, the level of technical and mathematical skills of those who need information decreases. This inverse relation is shown in the following image. It illustrates clearly the need for different approaches to providing information to different stakeholders. But before we explain the different approaches, we will discuss the mistakes that companies make by not following this path. Let me explain how we, as entrepreneurs, learned about them.

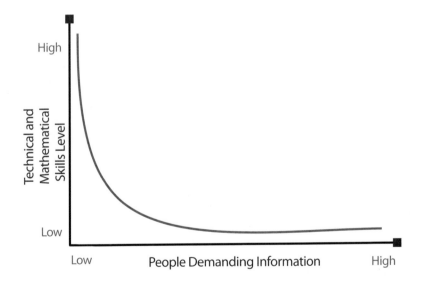

The inverse relationship between information demand and the skills required for self-service

The developers could build what we call today an InfoApp for any number of users to get answers to any number of questions. And these additional users did not have to learn the query language that we developed.

The Informational Application Was Borne Out of Customer Needs

As more and more people in the enterprise started to use computers and the FOCUS product to retrieve information, we started to hear more and more requests for new features. The very first improvement we had to make in our language-based product, FOCUS, was to allow the language syntax to be typed into a separate file, and that file submitted to FOCUS to be executed. The need for this should be obvious. If users are asking for the same information all the time, why should they have to type it each time? Users can simply use an already existing file and execute it each time they need new information. Today we call this reusability. Of course, if many files exist, then the files could be available to more than one person. Today we call this *sharing of BI assets*. Herein lies the beginning of an *application* that can be distributed to less technical users.

But there is a problem with this scenario. Not everyone may want the exact same information, but more likely each person would want to see slightly different information. We certainly do not want to have to issue a full English query for each variation that people may want. This required us to enhance the architecture with a scripting language that would be able to interact with the syntax in a file and parameterize it. In this way, users could use the basic structure and yet configure their request in order to get precisely what they need, or in other words, parameterization allows users to have a conversation with the data source in order to get the answers they need.

For example, if the filter was IF YEAR EQ 1976, we could change it to IF YEAR EQ &YEAR. Upon execution, the system would prompt the user to enter a value for YEAR. In this way, the same stored file could be used over and over again, but the answers to each query instance could be different each time. By parameterizing other aspects of the stored file, such as the columns, the sort fields, and anything else, we could control the application and allow each user to individualize it. Many refinements were added to this basic facility with the intent of allowing people who have no knowledge of the underlining language to still get to the information they want.

What we did was to enable personalization. In other words, every user could use the same file, but give it different parameters and get entirely different results. This seemingly small change had a profound effect. The essence of it is that what had been a self-service product for an individual user now has become a self-service tool for a *developer* to help other users get what they want. The developers could build what we call today an InfoApp for any number of users to get answers to any number of questions. And these additional users did not have to learn the query language that we developed.

This allowed enterprises to distribute information to many more users to improve decision-making. The demand for this type of information distribution grew rapidly, as the ROI from it was substantially larger than the ROI from individual self-service. Hence, the amount of future effort in the product development largely went not into individual self-service features, but to helping the developer provide more services to more people.

Self-service users who we thought we were going to provide with a powerful and simple query language for their own personal information needs, turned out to be self-service developers. In a few years, we had thousands of applications running on what today would be a very primitive environment.

Tailor the Experience to the Individual User

Today many end users do not use language to personalize the information that they want to receive. Instead, they use GUI controls to make selections with a click of the mouse or tap gesture. Sites like Expedia provide user interfaces so that the selection of parameters can be made with minimal input effort. One may think of Expedia as the perfect informational application that allows users to quickly find answers to travel-related inquires, such as airplane schedules, and prices. These answers help users plan a trip in a cost-effective manner, that is, it helps them make travel-related decisions.

A good UI makes each task obvious and thus does not require training.

As the Expedia example shows, the entire user experience (UX) discipline has evolved to make the passing of parameters in applications more user-friendly. It is built on top of the foundation that provides the technical architecture to pass parameters. Even the greatest UX designer will fail if the underlying architecture does not provide means for deep parameterization. But it took quite a while for the technology to evolve from language-based parameterization to what has become known in the BI and analytics space as guided user interfaces, and more generally as *custom application interfaces.*

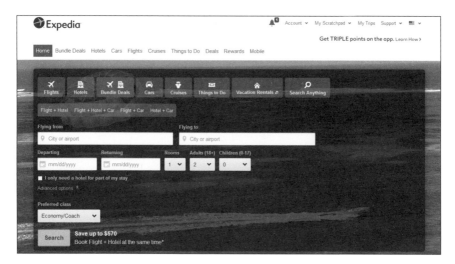

Expedia.com[17]

The site has a custom built UI and UX that makes it immediately obvious to visitors what they can do. A good UI makes each task obvious and thus does not require training.

The significance of this evolution is that both self-service and the delivery of information can be tailored to the specific needs and workflows of particular users. *Tailoring* creates an exact fit, as in the clothing industry. The tighter the fit, the more comfortable the user is with the product. Tailoring minimizes not only the time to learn a product, but also the time to actually use the product, that is, the time required to get to the information you want. This is why when timing is of the essence, a domain-specific application provides the shortest path to make a decision. The Expedia UI is dedicated to making travel decisions quickly. Notice in the Expedia screenshot how the UI makes it immediately obvious to users what they can do.

Imagine if the site was generic regarding any type of decision – let us say for travel, real estate, or car purchasing decisions. This would overcomplicate the UI and the time to get to the data needed to make a decision. This illustrates an important point. Self-service tools are generic, made for any type of analysis, while informational applications are domain-specific, meaning they are purposefully built for specific decision-making. The more generic the tool, the harder it is to learn, and the more time it takes to get through it to domain-specific information. Hence, the need and value for tailored informational applications.

The Informational Application Should Have Been Self-Evident
One could argue that the transition we described in the prior section should have been self-evident. After all, if we construct a pyramid of user skills in most organizations, it probably would look something like the one shown in the following image, and you can see that the non-technical users dominate the spectrum of users.

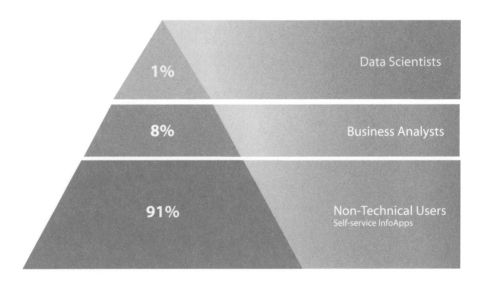

User Pyramid

Despite the large number of non-technical users today, much of the industry still focuses on developing tools for those skilled in the art of analysis. In the next chapter, we will investigate different types of users and the right approach for each one, in order to illustrate the point that self-service and information distribution have to be differentiated and used appropriately. We will focus on the differences between the different users and their needs.

Chapter Four

Different Users, Different Needs

We ended the prior chapter with the user pyramid. Here we will do a deep dive and discuss the users in each segment of the pyramid – their skills, their needs, and their decision-making styles. Nearly every industry uses a segmentation method to identify subgroups of customers and to tailor solutions to their unique needs. BI and analytics is a broad field with very diverse stakeholders, so it is necessary to segment and tailor the experience to each user type.

The Top of the Pyramid

Let us start at the top of the pyramid. This 1% of users is considered to be the cream of the crop. Many people refer to them as data scientists. In October 2012, Thomas H. Davenport and D.J. Patil published an article in the Harvard Business Review, *Data Scientist: The Sexiest Job of the 21st Century*[18], which explained how using data can transform the fortunes of companies. And they describe the origins of the term *data scientist* to describe the individuals driving such transformations.

The article tells the story of the "hockey stick" growth of customer acquisitions at LinkedIn®. It starts in 2006, when the company had under eight million users. The user base was growing linearly by user invitations and referrals. The growth pattern changed dramatically when a new employee, Jonathan Goldman, with a Ph.D. in physics from Stanford, started building algorithms that predicted which people were most likely to connect. He built a recommendation engine to present to users other

> BI and analytics is a broad field with very diverse stakeholders, so it is necessary to segment and tailor the experience to each user type.

users with whom they may want to connect. What adds to the "sexiness" of the story is that traditional product management was somewhat skeptical and against Jonathan's project. So he operated in stealth mode.

The article gained a lot of attention and the demand for data scientists grew astronomically, as shown in the following graph.[19]

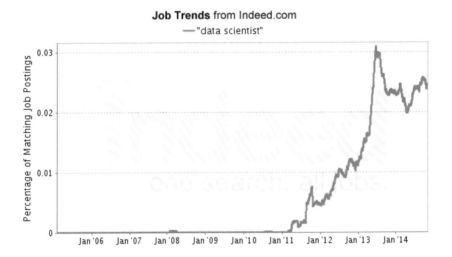

Demand for Data Scientists

With the increased demand also came fear about the shortage of data scientists in the labor force. A May 2011 McKinsey Global Institute report estimates that by 2018, "the United States alone could face a shortage of 140,000 to 190,000 people with deep analytical skills, as well as 1.5 million managers and analysts with the know-how to use the analysis of big data to make effective decisions."[20] According to the MIT Sloan Management Review survey, four in ten (43%) companies report their lack of appropriate analytical skills as a key challenge.[21]

Fear and confusion emerged in the market place, which in turn drove the salaries of data scientists up - a median base salary of $91,000 for a junior-level data scientist, and up to well over $250,000 for those managing a team of ten or more data scientists.[22]

Whenever a hype emerges, the best approach is to go back to basics.

To capitalize on the high demand, more and more people added fuzzy credentials to their resumes.

This led Davenport to write another article entitled, *It's Already Time to Kill the "Data Scientist" Title.*[23] Here he explains why he felt the need to write about killing the term he helped coin and popularize.

"Shortly after the article[24] came out, a woman introduced herself to me at a health care analytics conference. Her business card said Data Scientist, but it was clear that she was a quantitative analyst at best. 'Who can resist having the sexiest job of the century?' she asked."

Whenever a hype emerges, the best approach is to go back to basics. And that is exactly what Davenport did in his second article. He clarified the basic analytic needs and tasks so that people can better judge job candidates. Rather than looking at the title, people should focus on the type of analytic activity they need and find the appropriate talent based on that.

"You should also specify just what the job is going to do with the data. These categories might include:
- Statistical analysis
- Query and reporting
- Database administration
- Data warehouse management
- Data integration."

As you can tell, this covers the full spectrum of BI and analytics related tasks – from data management and preparation to various form analysis.

Following Davenport's task-oriented description, we can now say that the people in the top 1% are well versed in advanced statistical and mathematical methods, and typically have advanced degrees in one of these areas:

- Statistics
- Operations research
- Mathematics
- Computer science
- Economics

What do they do? They typically:

Perform research on complex topics – why things are happening, which things may happen, etc. These are often one off research projects to support strategic decisions. As in the LinkedIn example, Jonathan Goldman performed a lot of research to build the algorithms that made the recommendations. It must be noted here that his algorithm would have had little impact on the business unless it was operationalized. The operationalization of the results of analysis is a huge topic that we will tackle later in this book.

Perform data modeling – use statistical and data mining techniques to identify patterns in consumer behavior or events, or just to classify data. These models are used to execute marketing campaigns, to improve customer service, for up-sell and cross-sell, etc. However, the execution is typically handled by another group, for example, the operationalization is handed off to operational IT.

Perform on-going tuning and optimization – when models and algorithms are deployed in production environments, advanced analysts typically monitor the performance of the models. Model performance deteriorates because market conditions may change, human behaviors may change, or the demographic of the population may change. Any of these changes would affect the accuracy of the model, hence the need for ongoing tuning and optimization.

No tool can replace a good data scientist. Furthermore, since there are many statistical anomalies, the untrained users often become victims of various statistical traps.

What don't they do? As important as it is to know what the advanced quantitative analysts do, it is equally important to know what they do not do in order to be able to maximize the use of this valuable and rare resource. Advanced analysts neither build operational reports nor applications to operationalize their findings. The former is done by the business analysts, and the latter by IT and application developers. Directing advanced analysts to those tasks is not an effective use of their time.

The advanced analysts use tools like WebFOCUS RStat, R, Knime®, and SAS® Enterprise Miner™ to iteratively explore the data and build models. They spend most of their time working with such tools, and it frequently takes years of training and experience to get familiar with their intricacies.

Despite frequent hype about new tools that can do such complex analysis without any training, the reality proves to be somewhat different. No tool can replace a good data scientist. Furthermore, since there are many statistical anomalies, the untrained users often become victims of various statistical traps.

Given that, our recommendation is to always use a professional to perform the advanced analytics. From a value perspective, the value of advanced analytics is in their operationalization, such as embedding them in business processes for on-the-job decision support. Thus, the work can be meaningfully divided. The BI specialists can prepare the data, the statisticians can build the model, and IT can build the operational application. Under this division of labor, organizations can leverage their internal BI and IT teams to do the majority of the work, and outsource the modeling to highly trained statistical professionals. To give you perspective, 60-80% of work in deploying predictive analytics is in the data preparation. The BI experts, with the help of your IT, can do this part easily. This key to success is the proper allocation and coordination of resources, as shown in the following image.

Data Preparation

- 60 - 80% of total project time
- Use your BI and IT experts to prepare the data based on statistician specifications

Statistical Modeling

- 10% of total project time
- Use professional statisticians

Operational Application Development

- 10 - 30% of total project time
- Use IT

Resource Allocation for Advanced Analytics

The Middle of the Pyramid

The middle of the pyramid covers two categories of Business Analysts, which we will describe separately.

The Insights Analyst

The short supply of data scientists has created an opportunity to fill the skills gap with new emerging technologies. About 10 years ago, a new category of visualization technologies emerged that made it easier for business analysts to upgrade their skills without significant training and to start looking for insights in a variety of data sources.

A new term was coined to describe this type of analyst – *the citizen data scientist*. The term was coined by Gartner, and as one blogger describes it, "the idea here is that tools and technology have advanced to a place where everyday Joes within an organization can leverage them to perform analytic tasks that would previously have required the expertise of a highly skilled data scientist. In fact, Gartner recently predicted that between now and 2017, the number of citizen data scientists will grow five times faster than their highly trained counterparts."[25]

The rise of citizen data scientists, or *insights analysts* as we call them, reinvigorated the debate about self-service analytics because they use tools to access data and perform analysis themselves without the help of IT or other resources. The term citizen has a bit of a propaganda effect, as it is meant to signify the democratization of data access and the power of a do-it-yourself (DIY) approach, which in turn has created a new hype about how the new technologies can provide complete self-sufficiency. The belief that every business user can be made completely self-sufficient by using those tools has led some people to equivocate self-service with data discovery. This is a narrow view of self-service, as it takes into account how one user segment with very particular skills can become self-sufficient.

Naturally a different segment of users with different skills would require different self-service, for example, the statisticians that we mentioned in the previous section. It is easy to see that the tools for the upper 1% are very different from those for the citizen data scientists. Aren't they providing services for themselves, too? Similar differentiation of the self-service can be observed through the entire user spectrum, indicating that one approach does not fit all.

It is important to note that the tools may be the same, but the methods the analysts use can be very different.

Furthermore, many companies are beginning to find out that de-emphasizing the role of knowledge and skills can lead to incorrect analysis and conclusions. Even simple statistical anomalies related to averages can fool many analysts. As Xiao-Li Meng, Professor of Statistics at Harvard University, says, the Simpson's Paradox[26] is responsible for "a vast quantity of misinformation. You can easily be fooled."[27] Incorrect inferences from analysis are typically very costly. So, when crafting a strategy for BI and analytics, the hype has to be separated from the reality, and the technologies have to fit the skill sets of the targeted users.

What do data discovery/insights analysts do? They are typically charged to perform analysis and discover new insights that can generate new business by identifying new customer and market trends or generated cost savings by discovering the root causes for inefficiencies. If insights are discovered in a timely manner, they can create new opportunities for monetization by revealing new customer needs, new customer segments for targeting, emerging consumer behaviors and purchasing trends, etc. Time is of the essence in the business of discovering insights, since opportunities create competitive advantage only for a short window of time – until the competitors discover them. Hence, those types of analysts need a lot of flexibility to get the job done quickly. For this reason, they:

- Combine various data sources, both internal and external, to be able to glean new insights from a larger variety of data sets;
- Use visualization to explore the data quickly; and
- Craft stories to convey to the business decision makers the insights which they gleaned from the data.

What don't they do? The data discovery analysts do not operationalize the insights that they discover. This means that they do not build reports or applications to be used for decision-making by operational employees and users. Just because they use visualizations to discover insights that does not mean that their visualizations can be deployed to operational users to change their performance. Many people confuse the visualizations created by the data discovery analysts with dashboards, and deploy them to the disappointment of their users. The differences between those tools and the role that they play in the decision-making process will be discussed in another chapter.

The Business Analyst

This is the most misunderstood category of users in the BI and analytics industry because the term is a catch-all term, and catch-all terms introduce a different type of confusion, compared to terms like citizen data scientist. That means the skill level and the domain level expertise vary greatly among employees who have the title business analyst. Therefore, the BI and analytics strategy has to carefully evaluate the sub-segments in this category.

For the purposes of this book, we will distinguish between three types of business analysts: the SME/specialist analyst, the go-to analyst, and the implementation analyst.

Subject Matter Expert (SME) Analyst

The SME analyst specializes in a particular functional area of the organization. For example, there are marketing analysts, consumer insights analysts, financial analysts, logistics analysts, etc. The reason why they specialize is because the methodologies are different, and it takes years of training to get versed in each particular methodology. It is important to note that the tools may be the same, but the methods the analysts use can be very different.

To illustrate the difference, a marketing analyst can be very well versed in customer lifetime value methodologies, while a financial analyst may be versed in marginal cost analysis. It is quite possible that if you put the two analysts in the same room, neither one would understand what the other one is talking about. When formulating a strategy for BI and analytics, it is important to understand that difference, and also the fact that the different methodologies frequently do not require different tools. This is why most of these analysts use Excel or standard BI tools, like WebFOCUS InfoAssist.

What do SME analysts do?
- They perform routine analysis to monitor business operations.
- They perform ad hoc analysis to discover root causes when things go wrong.

> The emergence of this segment (shadow IT) is largely driven by the need of the business to get answers to pertinent questions quickly.

- They build reports and dashboards to be used by other people—typically executives and managers.

What don't SME analysts do? They do not build applications or information distribution systems. They do not perform any data quality or integration tasks or create reusable metadata for other people. But most importantly, they do not build reports and dashboards that have complex logic in them. Reports and dashboards with complex logic require multistep processing, that is, the ability to process queries sequentially, where each step is a query that becomes an input for the next step, apply business rules at each step, and generate a final outcome. To be able to build multistep reports requires special scripting technologies like WebFOCUS Dialogue Manager. Thus, those tasks remain in the domain of IT, application developers and the very advanced and technically savvy business analysts.

The Go-to Analyst

This type of analyst has become known as a shadow IT, as they have mixed skills. They understand data and can, in many cases, manage most data-related tasks in order to perform analysis quickly and deliver results to the business users. Like a jack-of-all-trades, they have a variety of data management and analytical skills that allow them to produce reports very quickly. This category has been the major driving force behind the growth of the self-service analytical tools, such as WebFOCUS Business User Edition.

What do go-to analysts do?
- They find various data sources that can shed light on particular problems.
- They negotiate with IT to prepare data extracts or views in the databases.
- They perform non-routine data preparation tasks.
- They perform ad hoc analysis on various topics.
- They quickly build reports and dashboards that they push to other users.

What don't the go-to analysts do? They do not build production applications, even though many of them collect and maintain complex personal databases to answer specific business questions. They also do not perform complex analyses that may require subject matter expertise. Sometimes they do double duty and act as implementation analysts, but largely they stay focused on supporting business users in an ad hoc fashion. The emergence of this segment is largely driven by the need of the business to get answers to pertinent questions quickly. On the other hand, the ad hoc fashion of their work often interferes with IT's ability to build and deliver the right applications to enable faster decision-making. Tensions between shadow IT and real IT have been flaring for a few years now. Better integrated ad hoc tools and app development tools can turn this tension into cooperation as the go-to analyst's work can be picked by IT and productionized.

Interestingly enough, the go-to analysts create both a bottleneck and an information overload in organizations. First, they create bottlenecks because they are the go-to person for ad hoc queries from the business executives and operations managers. Whenever anything goes wrong, the business managers turn to the business analysts for answers. This creates a significant backlog of requests, which interferes with the routine reporting. Second, since the outcome of all ad hoc requests are reports sent to the business users, over time this creates an information overload. The go-to analysts mistakenly believe that the more reports they publish to the business users, the easier it gets for the business users to get their own answers. Thus, business users end up having over 100 reports in file folders. But now they have to remember which report is useful to answer what question. Hence, this approach is wrong, as publishing more reports is not the way to address how business users can get answers to their questions faster and easier. A better approach is for business analysts to work with the implementation analysts and IT to rationalize the domain-specific questions into a single informational application so that the end users can get answers themselves.

The Implementation Analyst

The implementation analysts typically go between business and IT to negotiate the development of complex operational reports, dashboards, and informational applications, or they are the go-to person to answer any variety of data-related questions. This is a difficult and ungrateful job, as the implementation analyst not only has to translate between groups who do not speak the same language, such as business and IT, but also has to manage all the tension, such as when business wants everything done now but IT is severely constrained resource-wise.

What do implementation analysts do?

- Gather business requirements from the business users – what measures they want to see in reports and dashboards, what visualizations need to be used, how data should be formatted, etc. Very frequently, the analysts provide input and fill the gaps between what the business users state they want and what they indeed need.
- Gather data requirements for DBAs and system administrators.
- Work with IT to build the final specs, which frequently include data integration, security, data quality, front-end development, deployment, and maintenance.
- Advanced implementation analysts have the information architecture skills to consolidate multiple reports into informational applications for the business users to get their own answers.

What don't implementation analysts do? They do not perform analysis. Their time is best spent operationalizing insights and consolidating reports into easy-to-use applications for end users to get their own answers.

The Bottom of the Pyramid

Did you know that there are approximately three million analysts in the U.S. labor force?[28] These are people who have the word *analyst* in their job title. Of the three million, approximately 40,000 are statisticians and 70,000 are operations research analysts, that is, the total number of very advanced analysts (data scientists) is about 110,000.[29]

But what about the other 130 million people in the labor force?[30] Do they need information to make decisions? Interestingly, at least in my experience, these operational employees are never represented when purchasing decisions about BI and analytics tools and platforms are being made. There are two factors that contribute to this unfortunate situation.

First, there are some people who believe that not all employees make fact-based decisions that require access to information. Therefore, decision support is reserved for the executive and mid-level management, and is mainly done by SMEs and go-to analysts in an ad hoc fashion. There are many examples that illustrate the enormous effect on organizations when decision-making is empowered at the operational level, but let us look at just one.

WIRED magazine published an article entitled *The Astronomical Math Behind UPS' New Tool to Deliver Packages Faster*, which describes an app that helps truck drivers make routing decisions. The math is astronomical because of the number of possibilities from which the 55,000 UPS drivers have to choose. But even more importantly, the math is astronomical because of the huge savings when each driver saves just a little.

"$30 million – the cost to UPS per year if each driver drives just one more mile each day than necessary. By that same logic, the company saves $30 million if each driver finds a way to drive one mile less."[31]

You get the idea – help drivers drive one mile less by giving them a simple-to-use app. This astronomical math occurs in every industry once you deliver information to every worker. The Total Quality revolution at Toyota® and the Six Sigma transformation at General Electric were successful precisely because information was delivered to every worker to make fact-based decisions.

Second, it is assumed that the analysts who participate in BI and analytics platform purchasing decisions understand the needs of the operational employees and can make decisions on their behalf. But exactly the opposite is true. The analysts *assume that everyone else does analysis*, and therefore, they presume that the adoption of analytic tools is just a matter of company directive and training. Very few evaluations committees are aware of the extent to which operational employees are not mathematically inclined. *What percentage of Excel users can pivot data?* is a simple question that can stump the members of such committees. Once you recognize that less than 5% of Excel users can pivot data, people begin to re-think their approach to onboarding the non-mathematically inclined employees to BI and analytics tools. If employees cannot use the complex functions in Excel, how would they use the BI self-service tools?

So what do operational users do? They perform operational tasks – manage stores, drive trucks, perform repairs, perform surgeries, sell, purchase merchandise, etc. They do need information to make better decisions, but they do not do analysis. They need information to answer questions that arise in the process of performing their job duties. Car mechanics do not perform analysis on the replacement costs versus the repair costs of certain parts. But they need the facts to determine whether to repair or replace a particular part, a decision that can cost automotive companies millions of dollars, which we describe in the Ford story later in this book. The key here is that those users need quick answers to business related questions. Hence, self-service and information distribution have to be different for this type of employee than for the analysts, as we will discuss in the next chapter.

We would even stress that the approach has to be *radically* different. Hence, organizations have to adopt a more encompassing strategy to build organizational intelligence, rather than providing intelligence just to the executives.

Selecting the Right Approach for Each User Type

The majority of information consumers in today's enterprises is not mathematically inclined, nor needs to be mathematically inclined. When we look from a skills and needs perspective, we can clearly see that as the number of users grows, the mathematical and technical skill level declines. For this reason, across the entire spectrum of users, we cannot have one single approach. Instead, we have to vary the approach to meet the need at every skill level. Thus, the need for a robust and rich platform that provides a variety of professional tools and flexible approaches to self-service and information distribution to build a complete organizational intelligence system. The following graph illustrates how the approach and technologies change along the spectrum of users.

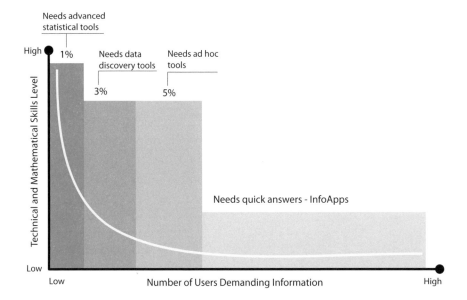

Aligning Technologies and User Skills

Chapter Five

Building Pervasive Organizational Intelligence

Two Different Systems of Intelligence

Intelligence is often defined as the ability to process information and make decisions. According to this definition, it is not only an individual activity, it can also be a collective activity, where groups of individuals process information and make decisions together or based on the inputs from one another. Thus, we can talk about organizational intelligence, or the ability of modern organizations to distribute the collection and processing of information among employees and to distribute the decision-making process. In turn, this makes organizations more efficient and effective, as it allows for a division of labor and specialization in skills.

Modern organizations are quite complex, and thus require different forms of intelligence to function efficiently and to compete effectively. The idea that there are different types of intelligence is not new.

For many years, decision researchers, psychologists, and behavioral economists have been arguing that human beings have multiple intelligence systems to process information and make decisions. Daniel Kahneman, a winner of the Nobel Prize in Economics, presents in his book *Thinking, Fast and Slow*[32], two highly specialized and functionally different systems in the human brain for information processing and decision-making. These very different systems fulfill different decision needs and are triggered by different circumstances. But the key benefit of having two systems is that by being different and by working together, they have made human beings more apt to survive and evolve.

System 1 Thinking, as Kahneman calls it, is automatic, instinctive, and emotional. It is especially beneficial when people have to make fight or flight decisions and do not have much time for deliberation. This type of decision making is often referred to in business as making decisions with the gut. As we all know, the gut is highly prone to errors. This is where System 2 Thinking becomes helpful. It is slow, deliberate, and logical. It allows the decision maker to go deep into the problem, gather detailed information, discern relationships and trends, discover counterintuitive issues, and so on. We call this analysis or rational deliberation. Despite being so thorough, System 2's major drawback is timing. By being too slow, it may cause us to miss opportunities or to fail to avoid danger. The key difference between the two systems is the timing of the decision-making. System 1 is focused on immediate payoffs, while system 2 is focused on long term consequences.

Organizations face exactly the same decision-making problem. They have to balance speed of action with error prevention. They do not want to miss opportunities and lose customers when it takes employees too long to research and make decisions. This is often referred to in business as analysis paralysis. On the other hand, organizations do not want employees to rely entirely on gut feelings when making decisions, as this will inevitably lead to errors. Hence, the objective of organizational intelligence is to build a distributed information collection and decision-making system that maximizes the speed of making decisions and minimizes error. Operational intelligence corresponds to System 1 Thinking and is most suitable for the front-line workers who need to make fast decisions. Conversely, System 2 corresponds to the work performed by various analysts employed in the organizations who investigate issues and trends by doing a deep dive into the data. The relationship between the two systems of thinking is visualized in the following diagram:

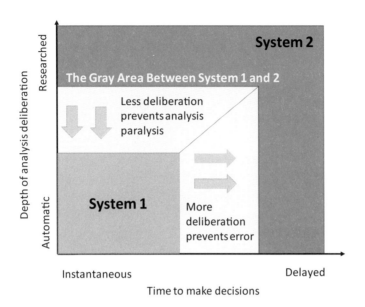

The relationship between System 1 and System 2 thinking

In the following sections, we present a taxonomy of the different intelligence systems and discuss how to build state-of-the-art organizational intelligence in order to drive better organizational performance. In Part 2 we provide case studies on organizational intelligence solutions and applications within the different categories of the organizational intelligence taxonomy that drive fast fact-based decisions among frontline employees, partners, suppliers, and customers.

Types of Organizational Intelligence

Business organizations are comprised of people and processes that are used to compete within particular market environments. Thus, an organization needs intelligence from its components (people and processes) and on its operating environment (market and competition). This allows us to break organizational intelligence into three distinct areas:

- Performance intelligence
- Process intelligence
- Discovery intelligence

Performance intelligence refers to information gathering and information processing about the efficiency and effectiveness of the organization. The key question to be answered by the information gathered for performance intelligence is whether people are performing to achieve the goals and to advance the growth of the organization, and whether they are making the right decisions. Its key objective is to help each individual in the organization to make accurate decisions and achieve maximum performance.

Since modern organizations rely heavily on a division of labor and specialization in function to achieve efficiency, they need intelligence about the processes that glue various jobs together to produce a final outcome. The key questions to be answered by process intelligence are whether the processes function according to expectations, and whether everyone involved in the process has information and makes adequate decisions. The key objective of process intelligence is to provide timely monitoring to prevent failure and to enable fast decision-making throughout the entire process.

Finally, organizations need intelligence about their operating environment in order to detect disruptive events, identify positive or negative trends, sense shifts in customer preferences, and foresee other events that may affect their business and survival. Furthermore, this type of intelligence does not have to be only externally focused. Organizational introspection and reflection helps detect internal shifts, anomalies, and inefficiencies. We call this type of intelligence discovery intelligence because its key objective is to discern external and internal threats and opportunities.

No organization can survive or gain competitive advantage without discovery intelligence. Without it, the organization will lose its relevance in the marketplace. Yet, discovery intelligence is not sufficient for survival or for gaining competitive advantage. Discovery intelligence provides insight and knowledge, but the benefits of knowledge can only be realized through action. Discovery intelligence has to be converted to performance and/or process intelligence so that the organization can act on the new knowledge. Organizational action requires an alignment of resources that can only be achieved through performance and process intelligence.

The following table summarizes the features of each type of intelligence, which we will discuss in detail next.

Performance Intelligence	Process Intelligence	Discovery Intelligence
Operational Reporting	Decision Support	Data Discovery
Financial/Sales Reporting	Monitoring (Dashboards and Alerts)	Search BI
Information Distribution (statements)	Embedded BI	Data Mining
Traditional Ad Hoc and OLAP BI	Operations	Machine Learning
The goal of performance and process intelligence is to standardize performance and drive organizational efficiencies.		The goal of discovery intelligence is to uncover previously unknown things.
90% of organizational activities fall into these two categories (to use an analogy, this is the engine and body of the car).		10% of organizational activities fall into this category (to use an analogy, this is the headlights of the car).

Types of organizational intelligence

The key objectives of the different types of intelligence and the connection between them are as follows:

- The key objective of performance intelligence is to help each individual in the organization make accurate decisions and achieve maximum performance.
- The key objective of process intelligence is to provide timely monitoring to prevent failure and to enable fast decision-making throughout the entire process.
- The key objective of discovery intelligence is to discern external and internal threats and opportunities.

Discovery intelligence provides insight and knowledge, but the benefits of knowledge can only be realized and monetized only through action. Hence, discovery intelligence has to be converted to performance and/or process intelligence so that the organization can act on the new opportunities and knowledge.

Delivering Performance Intelligence

As a broad category, performance intelligence is about the performance of people in the course of doing their jobs. But as the information is rolled up for groups, units, and divisions, it becomes intelligence about the performance of the entire organization. In turn, all functional areas in the organization require reporting.

Financial and Sales Reporting

The overall performance of the organization may be measured with financial and sales reporting. If sales is the lifeblood of every organization, finance is the measurement of the blood pressure of the organization. Frequently, financial and sales reporting are presumed to be a given and easy to do, but it still remains elusive to many organizations. There are a number of reasons for that, but let us focus on the two main ones: fragmentation and complexity.

Fragmentation is the result of the presence of many disparate systems in the organization that are not fully integrated. This can be due to the growth of the organization. For example, when a company grows through mergers and acquisitions, it acquires not only the business, but also the intelligence systems that support it. Fragmentation has many consequences, such as inconsistent data nomenclature and/ or bad data quality, and manual and ad hoc integration of report summaries that often produce data errors and other issues. Fragmentation leads to inconsistencies that severely impair the quality of the decisions about the health of the organization. But even more importantly, fragmentation obstructs the timeliness of decision-making when information from various sources has to be manually assembled. Any delay in monitoring the health of the organization results in a sunk cost, in other words, costs that cannot be recovered.

While fragmentation mainly affects the monitoring of the health of the organization, complexity affects the daily decisions of many employees. Complexity is a by-product of the emergence of multi-dimensional data, or the growing collection of

---

Operational reporting is about measuring performance at the front lines, where every decision directly impacts the profit and loss of the company.

more data points and more data attributes. It gives us an opportunity to learn why things have happened, but if done incorrectly, it overloads the user with information.

Consider a typical scenario of sales reporting in retail. Store managers need to know their sales. But today, retail data has many dimensions and attributes, such as product categories, product sub-categories, promotional categories and sub-categories. Naturally, some numbers in the sales report will trigger further questions. For example, if daily sales are down, a store manager may want to know which product categories caused the decline. Such questions are typically answered by analysts who prepare and give the manager another report. To reduce the burden on analysts, managers can refresh such reports on an as-needed basis. But as more and more reports are being created in this way, the result is a file directory with hundreds of reports. Now the store manager has to remember which reports contain answers to which questions.

This type of complexity is the unintended consequence of two factors:
- The desire of managers to know more about their business in order to make better decisions.
- The incorrect approach to solving the problem, that is, the creation of separate reports.

Instead, the solution should provide managers with an intuitive interface to create their own reports. It is easier to navigate a UI than to remember the content of hundreds of reports. We call this approach a guided ad hoc or an InfoApp approach, resulting in the creation of an intuitive informational application, such as the Expedia application previously discussed.

Operational Reporting

Operational reporting is about measuring performance at the front lines, where every decision directly impacts the profit and loss of the company. Such reporting includes logistics, supply chain, inventory management, equipment utilization, etc. The distinct characteristic of operational reporting is that it is very tactical and narrowly focused to support very specific job functions. Hence, it is essential that operational reporting provides decision makers with a clear and unambiguous view of operations, so that they can quickly make decisions.

Consider the analogy of a pilot's dashboard. The pilot's dashboard provides the pilot with necessary information to navigate the plane to a safe landing. It is designed to provide a clear and unambiguous interpretation of the facts. It is also designed to eliminate any distraction. For example, it does not allow for any analysis that may divert the pilot's attention from the main objective – the continuous operation of the plane. This idea is at the heart of the "Toyota Way"[33] of managing manufacturing operations. Principle # 7 of the "Toyota Way" states the necessity of using straightforward visual controls that immediately reveal the operating status of each manufacturing process without diverting the attention of the engineers to perform additional analysis. Thus, the key is that the provision of information should not distract the employee from the main task, which is getting the job done.

Ad Hoc and OLAP Analysis

Being tactical, narrow in scope, and supporting immediate decisions is what distinguishes operational reporting from ad hoc and OLAP analysis. In fact, ad hoc analysis has exactly the opposite characteristics of operational reporting. It is very analytical, as it aggregates performance measures across the organization. It also has a broader scope, and thus requires broader access to data sources and systems, and frequently is used to support long-term decisions. Ad hoc analysis is performed to discover root causes or to provide a broader picture of the organizational performance. It is typically performed by professional analysts using specialized tools such as WebFOCUS InfoAssist, and the findings are distributed to executives and managers via robust reports that typically include graphs and tables. Craig Kelly provides a good discussion on the differences between Operational Reporting and BI in his blog *Business Intelligence vs Operational Reporting vs Financial Reporting.*[34]

Perhaps the difference between operational reporting and ad hoc analysis most closely resembles the difference in function between Kahneman's System 1 and 2 Thinking. It is important to understand how the speed and scope of decision-making determines the type of reporting required. Tactical decisions have to be made quickly and without distraction. Strategic decisions, or decisions that require you to change operations, are taken slowly with a high degree of investigation and deliberation, and thus require professional analysts to work with various sources of information.

Information Distribution

Finally, there is information distribution, which is the ability of organizations to produce and send to various stakeholders, robust and detailed performance reports or documents. For example, investment firms send, on a regular basis, portfolio performance reports to their individual investors. The monthly bank statements, telephone bills, and energy bills are documents containing valuable information that users typically analyze to gain information about events and performance. What makes this category unique is the high degree of automation in the production of such documents and the scale of the distribution.

Massively distributed reports and documents are usually highly styled. They are typically distributed in PDF (Portable Document Format). But PDF is a static format. In 2006 we realized that most of the users want to analyze the contents of such reports and documents themselves. For example, an employee may want to filter out from a credit card statement his personal transactions and send just his expenses to the accounting department. This is not possible in PDF. An investor may want to rank his investments based on the return or the volatility. This is also not possible in PDF. To perform any self-service analytics on such documents, the user has to go to the issuer website and request a data extract that is typically delivered in Excel. The cost for the issuer is huge, as they have to maintain two systems – one for issuing documents and another for users to download the data. But it is also time consuming and cumbersome for users to perform the analysis in Excel, as they have to learn about functions and data manipulation. Some may not even have access to Excel.

To eliminate all these inefficiencies, we developed the Analytic Document Format™, (ADF) which allows you to embed interactive analytic features in every document. To use our previous example, sorting a portfolio is just a mouse-click or a tap. The preparer of the document can tailor the layout and the functions specifically to the user's skill set to provide the best possible user experience, which differentiates companies and ensures customer loyalty.

Finally, when implanting information distribution, it has to be taken into account that consumers today are device agnostic. They want a seamless user experience as they

A better approach is for business analysts to work with the implementation analysts and IT to rationalize the domain-specific questions into a single informational application so that the end users can get answers themselves.

move from their computers to their mobile devices. Hence, the distributed document has to be accessible on all devices. Also the interactions have to be specific to each device. In other words, the document has to intelligently recognize the device and adapt the UI for the particular device. This area has become known as responsive design, which is the ability of documents to change the design layout for each particular screen in order to make the viewing, reading and interacting with the document easier.

Information distribution allows organizations to extend the intelligence system to customers, partners, and suppliers in a seamless and cost effective way, in order to build stronger relationships and provide better service, as some of the customer-facing use cases will show.

Delivering Process Intelligence

The main characteristic of any process is that it is sequential. It involves a sequence of steps that have to be performed to achieve the desired outcome. Thus, process intelligence requires two things. On the one hand, processes are very tactically designed to achieve very concrete results, and so, they require within-process decision support. On the other hand, someone has to oversee the entire process, and therefore, processes require monitoring.

Decision Support

The within-process decision support is designed to support on-the-job decision-making. For example, when customer representatives are solving customer problems, they need access to the customer information, transactional history, products or parts availability, and other types of information which may reside in different systems. Thus, effective decision support requires access to information across departments. Only if employees can access information in a quick and reliable manner, can they answer questions correctly and make valid commitments to the customer.

Process intelligence applications are almost always custom applications for three reasons. First, the processes themselves are quite custom. Every organization builds different processes, and it is the uniqueness of the processes that makes organizations more differentiated and competitive. Second, providing quick access to reliable information across different functional areas in the organization is not easy. It requires integration. Third, the application has to fit in the workflow of the employee, and the UI has to be intuitive and tailored to how the employee solves business problems. Decision-support applications can be built entirely with an appropriate BI platform as custom applications, or alternatively, BI and analytics can be embedded via API calls in third-party applications to provide decision support. Embedding has become a popular method to quickly enhance process applications with information for fact-based decision-making.

Monitoring

Process monitoring has two characteristics. First, it has to be implemented on multiple levels, from tactical monitoring to overall process performance. Thus, it requires both real-time alerting capabilities and management dashboards. Furthermore, the alerts, reports, and dashboards have to be implemented against operational data stores, applications, or systems without a data warehouse. Since production systems cannot be slowed down, querying them for alerting and monitoring requires a highly specialized and optimized access to the data.

Visual design is also of the essence when it comes to monitoring, as the decision-makers have to get the facts at a glance. Any embellishments in the visual controls that may create ambiguity or the wrong interpretation have to be eliminated. A common example of visual ambiguity is the addition of a 3D effect and angle to a pie chart that may make a smaller slice look bigger. A second important aspect to consider is the parameterization of the monitoring dashboard. Like in the case of reporting, there is a monitoring dashboard overload. I frequently hear managers saying that they are getting more and more dashboards that make it harder for them to get the information that they need. Parameterization and customization give the users control over their monitoring needs.

Operations Research

Finally, operations research is performed in order to improve the processes through the application of advanced mathematical algorithms and modeling. As more processes are being digitized and more data is being created, this creates unique opportunities to leverage this data to perform analysis and optimize the processes. Process improvements occur by modifying the processes, by automating some of the decision-making, or by embedding advanced analytics in the decision-support systems to provide better insights to the decision maker. But it is important to note that the improvement can only take place if the results of the operations research analysis and modeling are operationalized and deployed within the operational processes. Hence, they have to be propagated both into the decision-support systems and to the monitoring dashboards. To make this process easier for organizations, we have embedded the open source R engine in the platform, so that any mathematical models created in R can be embedded with informational applications, dashboards, and reports.

Delivering Discovery Intelligence

Discovery, insight, and intuition are vital for both human survival and organizational survival. They are the starting point in the creation of new knowledge that, if put into action, transforms the lives of people and the operation of organizations. But discovery, insight, and intuition are still elusive, appearing to be more the by-product of happenstance and luck.

In his book, *Seeing What Others Don't: The Remarkable Ways We Gain Insights*[35], Gary Klein tells the story of Wagner Dodge, whose insight helped him survive the Mann Gulch fire (Montana, August 5th, 1949) and changed forever how we fight mountain fires. Dodge and 14 other smokejumpers were parachuted to the top of Mann Gulch to descend and put out a fire on a nearby hill. As they descended down the hill, an unexpected blowup (a sudden firestorm caused by the collision of fire and winds) trapped them, and the team had to run for safety back to the top of Mann Gulch.

Today organizations are trying to make the discovery of insight more systematic in order to avoid disruptions and to detect opportunities earlier.

Once the fire started, it gained speed very quickly soon travelling at 660 feet per minute, outpacing the smokejumpers and killing 12 of them. The insight that saved Wagner Dodge was that to escape the fire, he needed to start a fire in front of him. The new fire raced uphill and Dodge followed what is today known as the escape fire. He had invented a new tactic that changed firefighting.

The story reveals the true drama of what the author calls innovation by desperation. Had data been collected on the spread of fires and analyzed, someone might have detected examples of escape fires long before the tragedy occurred. But in 1949, such data collection was not possible.

Today organizations are trying to make the discovery of insight more systematic in order to avoid disruptions and to detect opportunities earlier. Innovation from desperation or invention by the flash of genius, as patent lawyers call it, is being replaced by systematic data-driven approaches to discern new patterns that may lead to loss or profit. Thus, various analytical methods and tools have been developed to empower the less trained in very advanced analysis in the discovery process.

The data discovery tools allow many business analysts to play with the data on their own without IT support, and to combine various corporate and non-corporate data sources to discover insights about the market and the customers. These tools provide means for analysts to glean into data sources that have not yet become part of the enterprise sanctioned data sources. Thus, they provide the means to scout the universe of data for interesting patterns and trends that may affect the organization. Unlimited exploration is what drives the adoption of these tools, and to help this type of analysis, we have added data discovery capabilities to WebFOCUS Business User Edition.

But the universe of data is populated with a lot of unstructured data too. Social networks produce unstructured data at a higher rate than the traditional transactional systems. While transactions tell us what consumers actually did, social network posts and conversations provide useful insight about why people may or may not do something. Discovering insights in posts helps create new products or improve existing ones. And so, Search BI and sentiment analysis for discovery purposes emerged. To satisfy this demand, we have created WebFOCUS Magnify and WebFOCUS Sentiment Analysis.

Today we are also collecting data at an unprecedented speed and depth of detail. This in turn requires more specialized analytical tools. This led to the rapid emergence of data mining, predictive analytics, and machine-learning tools and algorithms. For this type of analysis to be performed by statisticians and data scientists, we have created WebFOCUS RStat. Yet again, our focus and innovation was on the side of deploying the insights and formulas within InfoApps, dashboards, and reports, so that more people could be empowered with advanced analytics, without requiring them to become data scientists.

Performance and Process vs. Discovery Intelligence

Organizations have to allocate resources to their different intelligence systems. The question is how to allocate resources between immediate payoffs (performance and process intelligence) and future payoffs (discovery intelligence).

Organizations have to scale in order to maximize their market share and revenues, and scale requires standardization. Standardization also implies stability and repeatability. This means that processes are running as expected in a non-disruptive manner, and that jobs and tasks are repeatable every day and across all organizational units where similar jobs and tasks are performed. This ensures that employees can be trained to do tasks on a daily basis, and that all employees can perform the tasks in a very similar way and with an expected degree of competence. This is what we refer to as *running the business*, or in other words, performing routine tasks on a daily basis to generate revenues.

On the other hand, discoveries are by nature disruptive. As Hilary Mantel says, "Insight is when it happens, everything that happens afterwards is different. Insight cannot be taken back. You cannot turn the moment you were in before."[36] Gary Klein elaborates on how insights lead to transformation, "Our insights transform us in several ways. They change how we understand, act, see, feel and desire. They transform our thinking; our new story gives us a different viewpoint. They change how we act."

Since organizations need stability and repeatability to function efficiently, it should be clear that not all insights will be operationalized and that the insights that will be operationalized should be implemented in a non-disruptive fashion. The Japanese Kanban theory synthesizes an approach where the need for both stability and disruption coexists via a method of continuous incremental non-disruptive improvement. We summarized this relationship in the following diagram.[37]

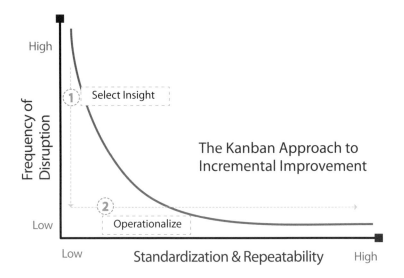

The inverse relationship between disruption and standardization

But many people today ask: What is the actual percentage allocation between the immediate pay-off systems and the discovery system? If I have to quantify it, the intelligence required to run the business should take 95% of the time and resources, while discovery should take 5%. This may seem counter-intuitive. But Herbert Simon, the father of information theory and a Nobel Prize winner in 1978 for studies in decision-making, provides a sound explanation. Consistent with Simon's theories, the degree of intelligence is measured by the degree of automation of the decision-making process, that is, making decisions with System 1 Thinking, and 99% of human decisions are automated, which is what allows us to function and survive.[38] Similarly organizations have to be extremely focused on performance and process intelligence to run their daily business, but also allow for discovery and for the operationalization of insights by integrating them into the performance and process intelligence systems.

Chapter Six

Data Monetization and Informational Applications

Data Is an Asset

There is an increasing realization in business that data is an asset. Some data advocates argue that it is becoming the most important asset and should be put on the balance sheet of organizations.[39] They compare the valuation of companies to the value of their fixed (physical) assets. The question then is how can we explain the huge gap between the value of the fixed assets and overall market value of the company? For example, how can a company have a valuation of $400 billion, but own fixed assets worth only $15 billion? We all know that intangibles such as know-how, branding, and customer knowledge are worth something, but we feel uncomfortable that we cannot assign a precise value, as we do to fixed assets. "This is especially troubling given that intangible assets make up approximately 80% of corporate market value."[40]

There is a growing realization that data can reveal the true value of both tangible and intangible assets, and thus, be monetized. Let us take a look at an example: customer data. WhatsApp® was sold to Facebook® for $19 billion dollars based on assumptions about the value of its customer base.[41] What is most interesting is that none of these customers were paying customers. So, Facebook bought WhatsApp for the opportunity to monetize its customer data. The key in this example is that it was Facebook, and not WhatsApp, that had an idea how to monetize the WhatsApp

---

The realization that data is an asset is leading many organizations to create a special C-level role – the Chief Data Officer (CDO) – to be the custodian of all corporate data.

customer data and was willing to pay a huge price for it. Why would Facebook otherwise pay a huge price for a company that has no assets and no revenues?

The realization that data is an asset is leading many organizations to create a special C-level role – the Chief Data Officer (CDO) – to be the custodian of all corporate data. The CDO has two primary duties. The first one is tactical – to ensure that all information is properly managed. That is known as the field of information management. Compared to other assets, information is unique because it has both a quality and expiration. In essence, data is perishable. Like physical assets, it can deteriorate over time if not managed properly. Email databases lose value if emails are not being updated and verified on a regular basis. Customer records get lost when customers change location. There are many more examples of how the value of data declines if it is not managed appropriately. The fact that information is perishable means that it can be monetized only within a short window of opportunity. Retailers know this very well, for they associate major lifetime events with direct sales opportunities. Lifetime events can be a newborn baby, a new house purchase, relocation, etc. Lifetime events present a limited opportunity to target consumers with the right offers.

The second duty of the CDO is more strategic. CDOs have to convert the data assets under their management into monetization opportunities. This is the hard part, as it requires the CDO to act as a line of business manager and to come up with new business models specific to making money with data. In the following sections, we will focus on those aspects of the CDO's role and more specifically on the different aspects of data monetization.

What Is Data Monetization?
In 2014, Forbes magazine published an article by Chris Twogood, *5 Essential Steps Toward Monetizing Your Data*.[42] It makes an important distinction between direct and indirect ways to monetize data. The direct way is quite simple – just sell the data.

Self-service informational apps are becoming increasingly popular among data brokers as a means to make it easier for their customers to select and purchase data elements.

> The power of information technology is in its ability to collect data on very small intervals across a large number of process nodes and turn this information into huge savings for companies.

There are two well-established business models in this area: data brokers and data providers.

According to a Deloitte® study[43] of use cases, data brokers use third-party data sources to create new data-based products. Companies like Acxiom® and Experian® purchase customer data from various providers and integrate the data from the different sources to create rich and accurate profiles. Then they sell particular data elements, such as email addresses, education, income level, and psychographic data, to advertisers and other companies who may use it to create targeted consumer offers. Data brokerage is becoming increasingly more sophisticated and easier to use. For example, Information Builders embeds Esri® maps in its BI and analytics products, but Esri allows customers to purchase third-party data to overlay the map directly from within Esri. As a result, an Information Builders customer who uses Esri maps can directly access such data and display it on the maps. Self-service informational apps are becoming increasingly popular among data brokers as a means to make it easier for their customers to select and purchase data elements.

On the other hand, under the data provider's business model, companies directly sell their own data to third parties, such as the data brokers discussed above, or the application providers who build data products from third-party data that they sell directly to companies and consumers. For example, many pharmacies sell aggregated or de-identified data to pharmaceutical companies to study patient adherence to medication protocols.

While the direct business models have generated a lot of interest in the past, the indirect models are becoming more important as they directly affect the fortunes of the companies who collect the data. Forbes lists three indirect models:

- Using data to make a process run more efficiently
- Using data to incentivize certain types of behavior
- Using data to reveal the true value of an asset

Let us look at each of these separately.

Using Data to Make a Process Run More Efficiently

If you were a logistics company, would you be interested in saving one mile a day per truck? For most people, one mile a day seems such a small number that it is not worth considering. To use the accounting jargon – *why bother with a number that is just a rounding error on the books?*

But is this true? Take 1 mile, 55,000 trucks, and 365 days a year, and what seemed a small number suddenly becomes a big number representing huge savings. This is the power of information technology at its best. It is the ability to collect data on very small intervals across a large number of process nodes and turn this information into huge savings. The logistics company that did this astronomical math to save one mile per truck per day is UPS, and it delivered $30 million dollars in savings per year[44], as we discussed in the previous chapter.

But UPS is not the only company to do this. Walmart® famously removed the paper packaging on deodorant to save just a few pennies per unit, which later on turned into a huge initiative to save costs, but even more importantly the environment.[45] Both the UPS and the Walmart cases point to something important. To realize these savings, you need something more than just the math and the data collection. You need the application that provides the truck drivers and the suppliers with information on how to make the decision to save a mile a day or a few cents on packaging. And the application has to be so simple to use that operational employees can make decisions at a glance and without any training. The savings from the Walmart initiative to cut packaging by just 5% are astonishingly high.[46]

Informational applications like the ones cited here allow us to scale seemingly small unit savings to huge savings.

Informational applications like the ones cited here allow us to scale seemingly small unit savings to huge savings.

Today, information application systems provide not only
immediate performance feedback, but also up-to-the-minute
information to support on-the-job decision-making.

Using Data to Incentivize Certain Types of Behavior

The concept of using data to change behavior is not new, but it is frequently underused.

During the early 1900s, the steel magnate Charles M. Schwab used data to increase the output and standardize the performance of his workers.[47] At that time dashboards did not exist, so he used chalk instead. As the story goes, his manager needed to standardize the outputs of the different shifts. The manager had used motivation, threats, etc., and nothing seemed to work. Charles assured the manager that this was an easy task.

He visited the floor just before the night shift came in and asked the daily shift how many heats they had produced. Then he wrote the number on the wall and left. When the night shift arrived, they asked the daily shift what the number six meant. The workers explained that the big boss asked them how many heats they had produced and that he wrote the number on the wall. Naturally, the night shift boosted its production and replaced the prior shift number with its own new record. Hence, a method of stirring healthy competition by displaying performance numbers was borne. Interestingly enough, the method achieved results that even the threat of firing did not produce.

Today, information application systems provide not only immediate performance feedback, but also up-to-the-minute information to support on-the-job decision-making. The latter is even more important, as it allows organizations to eliminate gut-feeling errors and to align the decision-making with best practices and fact-based knowledge. And yet despite their high impact and easiness to build and deploy, such performance benchmarking applications are not widely leveraged in the enterprise. This is quite puzzling, as such applications provide an easy way to monetize performance data that is already being collected by various ERP systems. The Ford Motor Company case study in Part 2 of this book provides a clear example of the benefits of such applications.

Using Data to Reveal the True Value of an Asset

Data can help us utilize assets more efficiently, and thus, extend the lifetime of assets, which in turn results in higher overall value. Let us look at predictive maintenance for example. Traditionally, there are three types of maintenance:

- Schedule-based maintenance (car service at 25,000 miles, 50,000 miles, and so on)
- Condition-based maintenance (when some event occurs, such as a warning signal lights up in the car)
- Predictive maintenance (before the condition occurs)

The first one is the traditional way of doing maintenance. In the absence of any data, you can only rely on past experience about regular wear and tear. But this is also the most costly, as many things can occur in the meantime. For example, the operating conditions may change, causing earlier wear and tear. The second approach is more data driven, and it essentially prevents unnoticed conditions that can lead to larger damage. The third approach is 100% data driven. By preventing a condition, it minimizes the risk of negative impact on adjacent parts. But it also avoids premature service.

Analogously, data-driven preventive healthcare aims to improve individual health, and consequently reduce the overall cost of the healthcare system. New health insurance business models are emerging that tie the individual premiums to trackable daily exercise goals. For example, Discovery Health Medical Scheme in South Africa gives members a free Apple Watch if they commit to certain daily goals.[48]

Those approaches to asset management and utilization rely heavily on the ability to collect and analyze data, and present the results in a timely manner to decision makers. General Electric is trying to reorganize itself around this business model with its Predix® system for the big internet of things, referring to the data-driven management of big industrial equipment.[49]

Data Monetization Framework

If we agree that data is an asset, then it should be managed as an asset. To borrow an analogy from manufacturing, value is created by turning raw materials into finished products. We call this managing the data value chain, or getting from data capture to monetization. The following graph illustrates the data value chain.

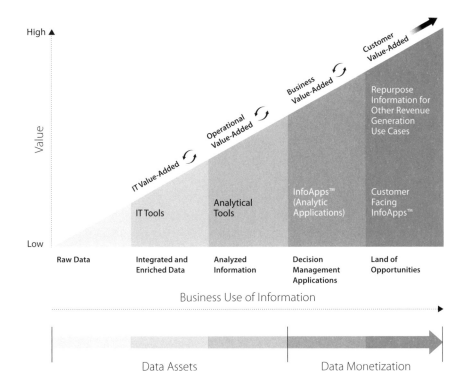

The path from raw data to data monetization

Similar to traditional manufacturing, each step in the process increases the value of data and gets us closer to the goal of monetization. The data value chain has two distinct products and distinct technologies to support each step in it.

It all starts with data capture, which involves many diverse technologies that have evolved to capture specific data types - transactional data, logistic data, marketing data, customer data, etc. The more integrated this data is, the more complete the picture. Transactional data combined with customer data can reveal patterns and trends that can be monetized in marketing operations. Like any asset, data has quality characteristics and thus requires special attention to maintain it. As the saying goes, "garbage in, garbage out" – if the raw material is of inferior quality, then the finished product will be of poor quality. All data is collected so that we can extract knowledge out of it. Hence, the need for analysis. Some people call the results from the analysis insights. The insight is the first product of collecting and managing data. Getting to it completes an important cycle of creating an asset. That is why we have labeled this section of the data value chain *data assets*.

The next section of the data value chain operationalizes the insights and thus monetizes the assets. This is the second product of the data value chain that actually delivers the monetization outcome, which is why we labeled this segment *data monetization*. As we stated in other chapters, insights create opportunities. But to realize the opportunities, the insights have to be operationalized. They have to be instantiated into either an operational BI application or a customer-facing BI application. The value of data can be materialized only by improving an actual decision process by using informational applications. The higher the potential loss or gain from a fact-based decision, the higher the value of the data monetization product. To give a theoretical example, how much would you be willing to pay for advice on a stock that will return 50% on investment? If your regular expected rate of return is 10%, then you can pay up to 40%. And so, that is the value of the data-driven application.

Most enterprises today do not manage data as an asset with a distinct value path. This is exactly why the role of the CDO is emerging. But most interestingly, the current 22% adoption rate of BI and analytics correlates directly with the first segment in the

---

Most enterprises today do not manage data as an asset with a distinct value path. Most organizations are satisfied with getting the insights and disseminating them as a verbal policy, rather than monetizing them through informational application products.

data value chain.[50] Most organizations are satisfied with getting the insights and disseminating them as a verbal policy, rather than monetizing them through informational application products. This brings us to the next section on the role of informational applications for data monetization.

Informational Applications Are Best for Data Monetization

We believe that the best way to monetize data and insights is custom informational applications (InfoApps) that allow the users to get fact-based answers to questions quickly. To achieve this goal, the InfoApps have to be built for a specific purpose and fit into a particular familiar workflow. The specific purpose requirement narrows the domain of the application, and thus, makes it easier for users to familiarize themselves with it. For example, Expedia is a domain-specific informational application that a user can easily use to get information and answers to all travel-related questions, such as flights, rental cars, and hotels. Contrast this with a general purpose tool for analysis. Such a tool can be pointed to any data set, but it requires the user to become familiar with the domain-specific data before being able to answer any questions.

The domain restriction and intended narrow use case allows the developers of the informational applications to fit the workflow precisely to the user's needs, and thus make it very intuitive to use the application to retrieve the desired information. For example, the layout of the application controls in Expedia makes it immediately obvious to the user what actions are required to retrieve information. This is not the case with general purpose tools, which have a standard workflow that is applicable to many use cases, but in turn require training and documentation.

These two features differentiate the informational apps from the general purpose tools. They give a different type of self-service. While the general purpose tools can free the end user from dependency on IT to get to the data, the purpose-specific informational apps free the end users from the need to learn tools. Users can retrieve information quickly and efficiently across different domains on an as-needed basis, without having to learn domain-specific data or tools. This makes InfoApps particularly suitable for operational decision support and customer-facing applications, where ease of use and speed of decision-making are essential.

Informational applications are different not only from the general purpose analytics tools, but also from analytical and monitoring dashboards. As the following example illustrates, an analytical dashboard reveals the facts and may show the root cause for particular facts. In the following image, the overall satisfaction with the call center customer service is directly correlated with the duration of the service calls. But the majority of the calls exceed the customers' preferred call duration of three minutes.

Analytical Dashboard   Informational App

What should management do? They can issue a policy requiring service calls to be kept within three minutes. But how do you track and enforce such a policy? In reality, when management issued such a policy, satisfaction declined even further, as many calls were abruptly discontinued at the three-minute threshold.

This points to an important factor that makes InfoApps so hard to conceive. Management has to come up with the incentives and measures that will change the behavior of operational employees in the desired direction. These incentives and measures have to be built into the informational application and tracked over time. Only in this way will the application guide the employees to make the right decisions.

The application on the right side shows not only the duration of the call, but also the customer satisfaction immediately after each call, thus preventing hang-ups at the three-minute threshold. It also provides additional status and benchmarking information to help employees self-assess their performance, as well as an interactive interface to get answers to any job-related questions.

Chapter Seven

Summary of Business Drivers for Different Types of InfoApps

This chapter summarizes the business drivers for the different sub-types of InfoApps within the three main types of organizational intelligence: process intelligence, performance intelligence, and discovery intelligence. Naturally, some informational applications fall into more than one of these categories. But for most deployments, one type dominates, or at least the primary benefit used to justify the investment in the InfoApp falls into one distinct category.

We have included these categories to help readers envision the many possibilities under the broad umbrella of organizational intelligence. Perhaps these descriptions will help you visualize what you can accomplish with InfoApps at your organization as well as help you justify the investment in data monetization opportunities.

Process Intelligence Applications

Operational Performance:

Key Drivers: Leverage information to improve employee decision-making and performance to save costs. The key business driver for implementing such applications is the direct cost savings.

Example: Ford Motor Company, one of the world's leading auto manufacturers, created an InfoApp that helps thousands of dealers resolve problems with warranty repair costs. Users can leverage 15 years of historical data to gather insights about manufacturing efficiency, supplier quality, and dealer repair trends. The application, described in Chapter Nine, saves Ford money by allowing mechanics and dealer managers to make better decisions at various stages of the automotive warranty process. Senior managers have greater transparency into their service and repair businesses, resulting in 40% fewer dealers being audited or entering Ford's global warranty counseling process.

Process Efficiency:

Key Drivers: Leverage information to make a process more efficient and to increase output. That typically means faster, cheaper, better. The key business driver is overall process improvement and an increase in output.

Example: Utz, a well-known snack manufacturer, created an InfoApp called SnackBoard that provides employees fast and clear answers to business questions related to sales, manufacturing, and finance. As explained in Chapter Twelve, people throughout the company use SnackBoard to drill into sales data via charts, graphs, reports, data visualizations, and other interactive methods, which has led to significant company growth, improvements in distribution and sales processes, and the ability to make more rapid decisions. The app allows the sales team to nimbly react to the daily business conditions. Tying daily production more closely to sales enables the company to streamline its supply of products, so the factories maintain just enough inventories for current needs.

Decision Support:

Key Drivers: Provide accurate decision support at the point of decision-making to improve quality of service and/or eliminate errors. Primary business drivers include: (1) eliminate the costs of erroneous decisions, and (2) improve quality of service to increase customer loyalty.

Example: First Rate, a developer and provider of portfolio analysis and performance measurement software for investment advisors and financial institutions, created an InfoApp called ExecView that helps wealth managers figure out how their businesses are trending (see Chapter Eight). The interactive app allows financial professionals to observe trends and filter data so they can get precise answers about portfolio trends very quickly. ExecView expands their decision-making capabilities so they can examine thousands of financial portfolios very quickly.

Loss Prevention:

<u>Key Drivers:</u> Eliminating loss is different from saving costs.

Losses can occur for many reasons and information can be used to reveal a potential loss and eliminate it. The main business driver is the need to eliminate fraud, waste, and abuse.

<u>Example</u>: iovation, an internet security company, maintains a knowledge base with information about billions of Internet devices, along with heuristics that help fraud managers determine the level of risk associated with online activities (see Chapter Fourteen). Interactive dashboards and InfoApps allow clients to examine millions of consumer transactions to circumvent fraud. 3,500 fraud managers in banking, credit issuance, e-commerce, online gaming, and other industries leverage iovation's fraud-prevention solutions to gather vital intelligence and correlate activities from suspicious devices in order to stop crime.

Opportunity Capture:

<u>Key Drivers</u>: Leveraging information to capture new or incremental revenues. Revealing timely opportunities in a business process allows employees to quickly capitalize on them.

<u>Examples</u>: nVision Global, a leading provider of services for freight bill auditing and payment, created an InfoApp to provide customers with up to the minute information on shipping routes, rates, logistics, and carrier contracts. As described in Chapter Ten, customers use the app to assess shipping options and make knowledgeable choices about their logistics operations, saving millions of dollars each year. The value-added service allows nVision to capture incremental revenue from domestic and international shipping operations.

Other organizations create opportunity capture apps to improve cross-selling and upselling activities, or to create a new revenue stream by selling information. For example, Moneris was one of the first banks in Canada to enable merchants to view their debit, Visa®, and MasterCard® transaction data online. They created an InfoApp called Merchant Direct that empowers customers to obtain a customized view of card payment activity and access consolidated statements and reports. Merchant Direct improves productivity in the Moneris call center and helps merchants manage information about consumer spending—all while boosting revenue for the company. See *http://www.informationbuilders.com/applications/moneris-self-service-bi* for the complete story.

Performance Intelligence Applications

Performance/Accountability:

<u>Key Drivers:</u> Improve and standardize employee performance and drive personal accountability in the organization. Key benefits are higher productivity.

<u>Examples</u>: Lutheran Life Communities, a nonprofit organization that owns and operates six continuing care retirement communities, created an InfoApp called Shipshape that allows managers to monitor employee performance and extend budgetary responsibility to individual stakeholders. As explained in Chapter Thirteen, comparative metrics enable benchmarking among all departments and campuses. Each user can see the relative performance of the activities under his or her purview, which helps the company manage food service costs, physician relationships, productivity, census mix, and more. Managers can monitor daily metrics, set clear goals, and create strategies for attaining those goals.

Applications in this category also help with regulatory compliance by helping senior officers fulfill a broad range of quality and revenue goals. Data can be rolled up from individuals to departments—as well as to divisions, organizations, and the entire enterprise.

Status & Alerting:

<u>Key Drivers:</u> Eliminate failures, omissions, disruptions, interruptions in services and processes, etc., as well as drive better customer experiences. All of these result in either financial losses or customer attrition.

<u>Example</u>: Farm Bureau Insurance, one of Tennessee's largest carriers of home and auto policies, relies on analytics to prepare for cataclysmic events, adjust resources, and contact re-insurers when major storms are expected to impact a large number of its insured customers. Real-time status updates alert managers in claims, accounting,

and customer support so they can maintain adequate staffing levels and prepare for expected financial impacts. Having increased visibility into claims activity greatly improves efficiency and revenue. (See *http://www.informationbuilders.com/customer/ farm-bureau-insurance* for the complete story).

Information Distribution:

Key Drivers: Provide comprehensive documents to a large number of users to give them a complete view of their accounts or business dealings. Improve the customer experience and eliminate costs associated with in-person inquiries.

Examples: U.S. Bank's ScoreBoard app, described in Chapter Eleven, provides information to large numbers of customers so they can track spending trends and better manage their purchases. This robust business tool allows 6 million clients to easily monitor credit card spending over various time periods. ScoreBoard improves customer loyalty and reduces overall support costs for the bank.

Principal Financial Group, a global financial investment management company, created an information distribution solution to reduce printing costs and increase the adoption of cost-effective online services. Its e-statement InfoApp enables millions of clients to view their financial activity in a fast, efficient, cost-effective way. They can change allocations, view investments, and drill into their transaction histories. Watch this video for more information: *http://www.informationbuilders.com/video/19018.*

Trust & Transparency:

Key Drivers: Provide full transparency and visibility into the operations of an organization, or provide the public or customers with vital statistics on particular topics of interest. Key drivers can be legislation, such as the Data Act, public health and safety concerns, and local government transparency. Business organizations can publish to customers the key performance metrics to boost investor and customer trust.

Example: Vantiv, a payment processing company, created a merchant portal that allows retailers to obtain insights that they can't get by analyzing their own point-of-sale data (see Chapter Sixteen). Merchants use Vantiv's customer-facing InfoApp to better understand the purchasing behavior of their end-customers, such as insights about their shopping habits and preferences. The interactive analytic environment boosts customer trust and confidence by demonstrating Vantiv's ability to meet their needs with targeted, high-value services.

Operational Performance Management:

Key Drivers: Establish organization-wide KPIs. The key here is to explain when organizations move from operational reporting to operational performance management. The driver is higher visibility into the health of the organization.

Example: Thyssenkrupp, a German manufacturing firm, created a dozen KPIs to formalize its procurement processes and measure progress towards strategic goals, enabling managers to measure the contributions that purchasing makes to the success of the company. These contributions are now clearly measurable and can be traced clear down to the resource level. For example, Thyssenkrupp can measure the financial impact of individual purchasing decisions on the bottom line, helping the purchasing department establish more favorable contracts and supplier relationships. (See *http://www.informationbuilders.com/customer/thyssenkrupp-ag* for the complete story.)

Discovery Intelligence Tools and Applications

Tools for the Professional Analysts:

Key Drivers: Analysts are primarily concerned with two things: (1) discovering the root causes of problems, and (2) gaining insights from data for new opportunities. This analysis leads to the discovery of hidden costs and revenue opportunities.

Example: Plex, an ERP manufacturing vendor, embedded a customizable analytic environment within its SaaS-based ERP system to empower customers to gather, visualize, and share information, as well as to analyze operational metrics and monitor manufacturing processes. Web-based design tools let people drag and drop data elements into custom reports, dashboards, and InfoApps, helping manufacturers understand every aspect of their businesses. More than half of the Plex customer base has adopted this powerful analytic solution, boosting overall revenue and solidifying customer relationships. (See Chapter Fifteen for the complete story.)

Embedding Advanced Analytics:

<u>Key Drivers:</u> Enhance the analytic capabilities in existing applications and thus save the costs of building new applications. The key benefit is that by embedding predictive analytics in operational applications, we spread insights to operational users who are not data scientists.

<u>Example</u>: Taylor University created an embedded BI environment that analyzes information about students, registrations, admissions, graduations, and other factors to predict which students are likely to continue into their sophomore year, and which students are at risk of dropping out. Taylor's predictive model spans the entire student lifecycle, from application and acceptance through matriculation and graduation. It determines the characteristics of those students most likely to successfully complete their studies, and identifies at-risk students that can benefit from the guidance of a college counselor to keep them on track—improving student retention rates. (See *http://www.informationbuilders.com/applications/taylor-university* for the complete story.)

Part Two

Case Studies

"The client thought they wanted a set of custom reports but
what they really needed was an interactive portal that would
help them get rid of paper and simplify crucial decisions."

Deborah Repak
Managing Director and General Manager
of the Products Group
First Rate Investment

Financial Services

Chapter Eight

Automating Portfolio Oversight and Compliance for
Wealth Management Firms

First Rate Investments

On January 7, 2015, Deborah Repak was talking with a couple of prospects when a
light bulb went off in her head. As the managing director and general manager of the
Products group at First Rate Investments, Deborah and her team have decades of
experience measuring portfolio performance and calculating rates of return. Sitting in
a conference room on that cold winter day, she realized that they could take these
analyses a step further.

"The prospects explained how they have to extract data out of their current system
to create complex spreadsheets, and then summarize it manually with Microsoft
Excel," she recalls. "It was clearly a laborious way to get to the information that they
were looking for."

It was just one of several important realizations that Deborah had that day. Since 1991,
wealth managers and financial advisors around the world have depended on First
Rate Investments to deliver portfolio information to their customers. The Arlington,
Texas-based company has created a web-based performance measurement solution
that reveals investment details for millions of portfolios. Knowing returns by account
is all well and good, but Deborah wondered how these clients could identify outliers
as they surveyed large groups of accounts.

"I was looking at their spreadsheets and I realized that they needed more than just a
new set of reports," she recalls. "What they really needed was some type of analytic

portal or app that would let them view their data from the top down– and then drill into exceptions based on whatever criteria they were looking for."

Deborah and her team didn't just want to extract insights, and they didn't want to have to crunch the data themselves. They wanted to develop a system that would make it easy for clients to obtain insights on their own. She later described it as the "a-ha moment" that launched a new and important business venture for her firm.

"It suddenly occurred to me that we had to shift our perspective," she continues. "The clients thought they wanted a set of custom reports but what they really needed was an interactive portal that would help them get rid of paper and simplify crucial decisions."

In other words, these prospects didn't just need a system that could respond to queries and spit out data. They needed interactivity so they could see trends and filter data to get answers. "They didn't just need to expand their information-access capabilities," Deborah adds. "They needed to expand their decision-making capabilities."

Expanding the Horizon of Possibilities

Ideas like the one Deborah Repak had that chilly winter afternoon can make fortunes, launch companies, and even disrupt entire industries. But it takes more than just a good idea to change the direction of a company or business unit. She had to produce a solid business case and sell it to management.

Consider the context. First Rate has gained a solid foothold in the wealth management space the old fashioned way: by crunching data, lots of it. They have built a prosperous business around reporting on data points for wealth managers and broker dealers—either one account at a time or for selected groups of accounts. Each evening after the market closes they receive holdings and transactional records for more than one million accounts. They use iWay integration technology to move the data into their systems and they use WebFOCUS to generate performance-return records for each holding, asset, and style class in each account. On average this involves building and storing more than 750 million account-return records in about six hours, which works out to 35,000 returns per second.

Could they use this data as the foundation of an InfoApp that reveals macro trends in accounts, sectors, and entire markets?

"We are sitting on a treasure trove of information in our databases, and we asked ourselves: How can we help our clients glean insight from all of this data?" Deborah recalls.

The answer came with an InfoApp called ExecView that transforms this massive data set into informational data points that help clients figure out how their businesses are trending. Here is Deborah's story—a tale of frustration, illumination, and finally, success—and one that reveals much about the gears that move the machinery of the investment industry.

Gaining Buy-In from the Team

Deborah Repak has been part of First Rate since its inception. As general manager, her responsibilities include leading the technical team in all product research and development initiatives and working directly with sales and marketing to drive business line growth. As a managing director, she is directly involved in the strategic direction of the company.

To turn her vision for ExecView into reality, she not only had to obtain high-level buy-in from her fellow senior staff members; she also had to convince her product team that the opportunity was worth pursuing—along with all the other things they were already working on.

"It's not always easy, but ultimately good ideas prevail," she says. "We identified a pressing problem—we have many clients in this same situation. They are mining tons and tons of data, and now we could offer them a solution that makes their lives easier."

The central tenet of the vision was simplicity: greater ease of use would mean less data mining, no tedious analysis, and no ad hoc reporting. With an InfoApp, you simply get the answers you need.

One of the reasons these simple apps are so powerful is that they embody the knowledge of many experts. Deborah worked with the Products team and the client

"The clients thought they wanted a set of custom reports but what they really needed was an interactive portal that would help them get rid of paper and simplify crucial decisions."

---

to refine the concept and create a proof of concept, which became the basis for developing a minimum viable product. Curt Graham, John Watkins, and other members of the Products team supplied subject matter expertise and technical know-how to build a self-service portal with WebFOCUS.

"We iterated back and forth with several clients to create the ExecView portal," Deborah recalls. "This is where WebFOCUS really shines."

Once First Rate's existing clients saw the first iteration of this new InfoApp, the real excitement began. They especially loved the power and control that comes from being able to get answers themselves, without getting bogged down in data analysis.

"They thought of lots of ways to view the data," Deborah reports. "For example, 'Show me all the fees I've collected for this set of accounts' or 'Show me the top 10 holdings across selected domains.' There were numerous questions they could suddenly answer with this self-service application."

Reigning in the Outliers

ExecView evolved based on enthusiastic insight from the team. What began as a customized product for one client quickly turned into a general-purpose product that First Rate could sell to broker dealers and other types of financial services companies. This is another common offshoot of a new InfoApp: Ease-of-use leads to more user requests and thus expansion of the capabilities of the app.

In many cases, ease-of-use leads to monetization as well. As of this writing, First Rate has sold ExecView to eight clients and its reputation is spreading fast.
"We are getting new prospects like crazy," Deborah exudes. "Our competitors don't have a tool like this. We can identify risk and return outliers in a very fast and efficient way."

For example, an investment firm can use the ExecView app to determine what may be driving increased revenue through fees, or look for areas where accounts and assets under management (AUM) may be decreasing. It allows them to run checks-and-balances on individual investment accounts and to fix accounts that are out of line (see figure).

ExecView also helps prevent issues with regulatory agencies regarding trading regulations, cash management, and diversification. Output can be stored, and the tool's export function can be used to verify the oversight process during an audit.

All types and sizes of financial firms can benefit from ExecView, whether they are managing 200 accounts or 2 million. Users include individual registered investment advisors (RIAs), oversight officers, and regional officers who manage or oversee large groups of accounts.

First Rate's versatile system can scale with the data without compromising functionality. This is the hallmark of a well-designed InfoApp: it simplifies complex processes and speeds up the process of attaining insights via self-service techniques.

Resolving Compliance Complications

ExecView helps wealth management firms comply with Securities and Exchange Commission (SEC) and Financial Industry Regulatory Authority (FINRA) requirements by shedding light on trends and practices that might otherwise be overlooked. Data visualization techniques within the InfoApp make it easy to absorb the data, detect pertinent trends, and take appropriate action.

One common scenario involves portfolio oversight. A client might identify a group of 50 accounts that are over-valued in equities and under-valued in fixed-income securities (see figure). The oversight officer needs to be able to instantly drill into these accounts and notify the pertinent investment managers that they don't comply with corporate policy.

"ExecView helps managers spot outliers based on each firm's unique business rules and strategies," Deborah explains. "These high-level views span groups of accounts based on a flexible set of criteria, such as by risk model, investment strategy program, officer, advisor, region, bank, and many other demographics."

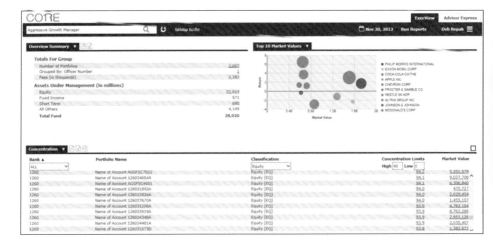

As First Rate quickly learned, InfoApps have become immensely popular within the realm of decision support because they excel at improving customer experiences and enhancing decision-making processes. Most importantly, InfoApps help users at the point of decision, whether that entails improving the quality of a service, minimizing errors, or supplying instant insight to move a process forward. The goal is to eliminate the cost of erroneous decisions and increase customer loyalty.

For example, if a customer support representative can quickly retrieve all the relevant information about a customer—while servicing that customer—then the app will improve the customer experience. This same philosophy applies to logistics decisions, purchasing workflows, supply chain management procedures, and many other domains.

Investment oversight is a case in point. Not all wealth management firms have efficient, well-defined, error-proof review processes. They need to be able to automate the discovery of exceptions and outliers from stated policies to bring portfolios, managers, and investment programs into alignment with today's stringent financial regulations. ExecView helps them look for areas where AUM may be increasing or decreasing, as well as keep a record of accounts violating the rules of risk management, cash management, and diversification.

Consider a broker dealer that is managing a book of business that includes 30,000 portfolios. Previously it took a lot of manual data extraction, data manipulation, and spreadsheet analysis for that firm to calculate summary statistics, rate distributions, risk returns, and standard deviations.

"We're talking huge spreadsheets, home-grown Access databases, and lots of tedious data extractions to accomplish anything similar to what we have automated with ExecView," Deborah says.

ExecView summarizes that data so the broker can follow unique paths of inquiry. Users have up-to-the-minute statistics on what is happening across a broad set of accounts. Previously, they either couldn't get that information or it was stale, manual, and fraught with errant calculations.

According to Deborah, is difficult to create risk-return reports with standard deviations across tens of thousands of accounts, but ExecView can create these reports within seconds. That's a game changer for oversight officers who are responsible for a group of investment managers or a group of accounts. Compliance and oversight are also important as financial services companies respond to regulations governing how their financial software is created and used.

Quantifiable Gains in Efficiency and Revenue

One of First Rate's clients used to spend a lot of time creating concentration reports that identify accounts that are holding more than 40 percent cash in their portfolios. Deborah recalls the "eureka moment" when this client first got a hold of ExecView. "When they saw how ExecView could automate these inquiries, they told us it would save 30 hours per month for anybody involved in these routine activities. There was such an obvious peace of mind, like a burden had been lifted off of them."

"Look for opportunities to transform data into meaningful information that makes someone's life better."

ExecView is also a "foot in the door" for prospective clients that may have their own reporting engines. "From a monetization standpoint, ExecView has resulted in a 10 percent uptake in our revenue per year as a value-added service," she adds. "This tool gives them management oversight, even if we're not the vendor who is providing their reporting solution. That's an exciting avenue into new client relationships."

When asked if she has any words of wisdom to share with colleagues facing similar analytic challenges, Deborah is quick to respond. "Look for opportunities to transform data into meaningful information that makes someone's life better," she sums up. "The joy we have experienced as a team in knowing that our solutions are giving our clients greater transparency and the ability to make intelligent decisions is really amazing. It feels good to know you have built something of value and that you're able to grow your own business while you're also helping your clients be successful."

Go Further

"We're accessing the same data as before, but we are presenting it and visualizing it in new ways. This speaks to the longevity of WebFOCUS and the power of analytics to continually provide answers to new questions."

Jim Lollar
Business Systems Manager, Global Warranty Operations
Ford Motor Company

Automotive

Chapter Nine

Analyzing Warranty Performance to Reduce Costs

Ford Motor Company

One hundred and thirteen years ago, Ford Motor Company unveiled the world's greatest contribution to manufacturing: the first moving assembly line. By reducing the money, time, and manpower needed to build cars, Henry Ford gradually dropped the price of his iconic Model T from $850 to less than $300, making high-quality automobiles accessible to the masses. Before long, Ford's automated assembly lines were turning out a Model T every 24 seconds, and by 1927 Ford had sold more than 15 million vehicles worldwide.[51]

Just as the moving assembly line changed the business model for building cars, Ford has fostered paradigm-changing breakthroughs in many other domains, including the modern analytic technology that has become a mainstay of the company's business. Ford's highly automated operation is largely controlled by information technology, both in its assembly lines and in the management tools it uses internally and distributes to its vast network of dealers.

For example, Ford's Warranty Operations group uses WebFOCUS to analyze repair efficiency, dealer warranty cost performance, and other stats that enable the company to build better vehicles and maintain happier customers.

"Dealers that used to wrestle with issues about warranty costs can now focus on providing a superior consumer experience in the service department," says Jim Lollar, Business Systems Manager of Global Warranty Operations. "WebFOCUS has advanced our capabilities substantially—it is a big leap forward in our ability to give dealers information."

Lollar is responsible for maintaining and enhancing the Global Warranty Measurement System (GWMS), an analytic app that helps thousands of Ford and Lincoln dealers monitor warranty repair costs and claiming trends. As a 34-year veteran of Ford Motor Company, he has been with the company through six generations of Ford Mustangs—and countless other vehicles as well. He describes GWMS is a customer-facing analytic app that empowers dealers to monitor their warranty repair costs and claim trends. Interactive charts, graphs, and dashboards allow dealers to compare their warranty performance against other dealers based on statistical differences and dollar amounts.

In addition, Ford uses GWMS internally to ensure that critical repairs are conducted in a timely fashion. With so many electronic systems on board today's cars and trucks, this foresight is especially valuable for software updates. Finally, analyzing this data helps the company gauge if the dealer network is on track to meet Ford's goals for effective and efficient service.

A Better Way Forward

Previously Ford dealers had to wade through lengthy tabular summaries to determine how their warranty-claim practices compared to those of other Ford dealers. Ford wanted to empower dealers to visualize and interact with this data through intuitive charts and graphs. If they made it easy enough and powerful enough, they knew they could help thousands of dealers identify and resolve problems with warranty repair costs, which would ultimately improve Ford's bottom line.

The development team confronted a complex IT environment that included several legacy systems and 15 years of historical data. They needed to transform this aging infrastructure to bring it into the modern age. Over the years this transformation has

"We have always had data on actual costs but we weren't giving it to dealers," says Jim. "We were giving them comparative statistics that were difficult to interpret. Now we can show them how they compare monetarily to other dealers within their measurement groups for each type of repair, and we can make automatic adjustments for labor rates and parts mark-ups."

taken place in several phases—most recently by creating purpose-driven, domain-specific InfoApps that empower business users to easily analyze manufacturing efficiency, supplier quality, and dealer repair trends.

WebFOCUS InfoApps such as the GWMS-EZ take information that was formerly displayed in rows and columns and present it in interactive charts and graphs, which are simple to use and instantly accessible. These real-time displays of each dealer's warranty business leverage three essential warranty metrics that Ford has tracked for nearly 15 years: cost per vehicle serviced, repairs per 1,000 vehicles, and cost per repair (see figure).

"We have always had data on actual costs but we weren't giving it to dealers," says Lollar. "We were giving them comparative statistics that were difficult to interpret. Now we can show them how they compare monetarily to other dealers within their measurement groups for each type of repair, and we can make automatic adjustments for labor rates and parts mark-ups."

This type of InfoApp is commonly referred to as an operational performance app since the key driver is a desire to improve employee decision-making and reduce costs. GWMS EZ allows technicians and dealers to follow best practices for repairs and to make knowledgeable decisions at each stage of the warranty claims process. Lollar

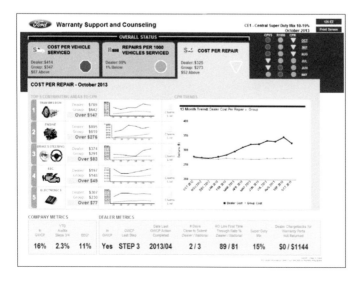

"We're accessing the same data as before, but we are presenting it and visualizing it in new ways. This speaks to the longevity of WebFOCUS and the power of analytics to continually provide answers to new questions."

coined the term "zero-click BI" to refer to this type of analysis. Just like looking at the dashboard in your car, the InfoApp reveals important metrics at a glance.

For example, when general managers access the Warranty Report, which is typically embedded in a Dealer Sales dashboard, they see a high-level summary, defaulted to the metric they have previously selected. These dashboards can be rendered on mobile devices, a useful feature as more dealers use tablets and smartphones throughout their businesses.

Gaining Buy In From Management

Innovative ideas are plentiful at Ford Motor Company, but turning nascent concepts into working prototypes requires management buy-in, team collaboration, and a compelling business case. Lollar sold the concept for GWMS by explaining how dealerships would gain visibility into their warranty repair performance. Each dealer's performance could be compared to a "measurement group" consisting of similar dealers in that region. For example, dealers could track the number of days it takes their shops to submit a claim after a repair order has been closed. They could easily see how their performance compared to their measurement group as well as to the national average. Other valuable feedback would include the percentage of claims that are paid without being returned for correction and dealership chargebacks for warranty parts not returned.

While this level of analysis usually requires dealers to install complex software—which complicates the IT infrastructure and drives up deployment costs—Lollar pointed out how WebFOCUS could deliver this level of powerful interactivity through a simple web browser—then later through mobile apps on phones, tablets, and personal computers.

Once management gave the Warranty Operations team the green light to proceed, the user community quickly got on board. Dealers now use an InfoApp called GWMS EZ to analyze performance and develop process-improvement plans. Interactive dashboards let them drill into details, such as 13-month trending graphs that reveal comparative performance for key warranty metrics. They can drill all the way down to individual claims in up to five repair categories. This level of transparency helps them keep costs down and comply with regional averages. With a couple of clicks service managers at each dealership can see how their warranty repair costs compare to other dealers. A "Top 5 Categories" button spotlights component groups that are most likely to raise costs.

These analytic assets are now in production with thousands of dealers around the world. Providing these new BI apps, in conjunction with changes to the measurement methodology, has allowed Ford to save tens of millions of dollars per year in covered warranty expenses. Ford reduces costs while its dealers can instantly identify anomalies and isolate problems.

Pushing into New Domains
In the fifteen years since the first iteration of GWMS went online, the system has steadily improved. Today's InfoApps are as different from the original 126 report as a 2016 Shelby GT350 is different from a 1986 LX Hatchback. Thousands of dealers have gravitated to the system because it is so easy to use. They simply click on a graph to drill down into the data, moving from the average cost of repairs or the number of repairs per vehicles serviced, to charts, to data showing repairs by components such as engines, transmissions, suspensions, and electronic systems. The analytic system uses standard deviation—a way of comparing the "normal" range of deviation to the average—to measure the relative performance of participating dealers. Ford has defined five statistical condition codes to determine how well a dealer is doing.

"The big picture is clear immediately if a dealer's warranty profile is out of line," Lollar says. "We provide tools and consulting services to help dealers ensure that their repair shops are running optimally."

Ford continues to derive long-term value from its BI investments, thanks in part to the ability of WebFOCUS to adapt to evolving business requirements. The core analytic logic that powered the original warranty reporting system still serves as the engine for the current iteration of these apps. WebFOCUS has evolved to include advanced capabilities for performance management, mobile analytics, data visualization, and statistical modeling, enriching Ford's analytic investments accordingly.

Soon, the GWMS InfoApp will include a new series of advanced metrics to help Ford deliver additional information to general managers. A big data project currently underway with Ford's Global Data, Insights and Analytics group will help predict what each type of repair will cost before vehicles are brought in for service. "The data set is immense," says Lollar. "It contains claims data from thousands of dealers that have performed millions of repairs over more than a decade. Each claim contains more than 30 attributes."

Ford used the open source R language to create predictive models that analyze warranty claims data. Lollar and his team are in the process of creating new dashboards that will allow people to visualize this data to identify cost discrepancies, and then suggest the likely causes of those discrepancies. For example, does the dealer in question service a lot of big trucks? Do they perform a lot of fleet repairs for companies that run their vehicles day and night? Have they been asked to repair an above average number of vehicles with a known transmission problem?

"All of these factors can be considered and adjusted using our big data models," says Lollar. "Dealers can ask themselves what they could have done differently to bring their repairs into acceptable cost ranges. We can provide data from thousands of similar repairs on similar vehicles, complete with all pertinent details including labor hours, part numbers, costs—and even unstructured data such as customer comments, service advisor comments, and technician comments."

For example, using its R engine and big data models, Ford can properly understand the impact of fleet repairs, which can be very costly for dealers. The model can then adjust the performance metrics to align for a standard vehicle/repair mix.

"We want dealers to be able to confidently take care of any customer that drives into the service bay. That means removing any hesitancy that they might have to take on risky or expensive repairs, such as servicing a fleet or cab company, because they fear it will negatively skew their warranty costs. Our big data project helps remove those concerns."

Big data analytics will also help Ford to proactively offer advice on how dealers can improve their repair records based on best practices discovered through thousands of similar repairs.

"Everything revolves around big data numbers now," Lollar concludes. "We're accessing the same data as before, but we are presenting it and visualizing it in new ways. This speaks to the longevity of WebFOCUS and the power of analytics to continually provide answers to new questions."

"We wanted to make clients self-sufficient by adding more advanced analytical functionality, better drill-down capabilities, and a more elegant user experience. We already had processing metrics and report cards that allow customers to monitor shipping activity. But they were hungry for more visibility into their data."

Luther Brown
Chief Executive Officer
nVision Global

Logistics

Chapter Ten

Capturing Incremental Revenue From Domestic and
International Shipping Operations

nVision Global

Moving freight around the world is big business. Modern trade agreements have paved the way for a global exchange of goods and services on an unprecedented scale. For example, between 1980 and 2015, the deadweight tonnage of container ships grew from about 11 million metric tons to around 228 million metric tons.[52]

For Luther Brown, chief executive officer at nVision Global, helping clients ship freight accurately and economically depends on the movement of a much more fluid commodity: information. nVision has evolved from a regional North American freight payment company to one of the world's fastest growing providers of global freight audit, payment, and logistics services. 168 companies worldwide trust nVision to audit, process, and pay their freight invoices—for all modes of transportation. nVision processes 100 million invoices and manages $5.2 billion in freight liability each year.

If success in business is a combination of luck and instinct, then Luther Brown found himself in the right place at the right time. At the beginning of the 21st century, when nVision was gaining traction, he saw how the internet could allow a frictionless exchange of information and ideas among original equipment manufacturers, contract manufacturers, resellers, retailers, and dealers. Buoyed by the complementary trends of outsourcing, globalization, and lower trade barriers, nVision was there to help companies move the goods. As Thomas Friedman aptly described in his best selling business title of that era, *The World is Flat*, Luther saw how a flattened world with open trade routes would quickly revolutionize the shipping industry. "We saw the future of global supply chains and we started building

"We wanted to make clients self sufficient by adding more advanced analytical functionality, better drill-down capabilities, and a more elegant user experience," Luther recalls. "We already had processing metrics and report cards that allow customers to monitor shipping activity. But they were hungry for more visibility into their data."

longstanding partnerships to take advantage of this constantly changing business landscape," he notes.

Luther and his colleagues got one important thing right: for logistics companies, competing effectively is all about moving data. And not just moving it, but analyzing it, visualizing it, and exchanging it among trading partners. Based on this simple premise, they parlayed their success auditing invoices into a value added service that quickly set nVision apart from its competitors. This service has resulted in a steady influx of new clients—and we're not talking about pocket change here. nVision's typical client spends between $20 million to $400 million on shipping per year and initiates more than one million transactions.

Today, hundreds of companies use the *nVision Supply Chain Suite* to streamline domestic and international shipping transactions, saving money on nearly every bill they audit. An important part of this suite is an InfoApp called iFocus Supply Chain Analytics that enables customers to optimize their supply chains and minimize transportation costs by analyzing invoice data.

Follow the Data

Here's how the iFocus service works. As nVision audits each freight invoice it extracts hundreds of data points. The company combines the data in unique ways to create operational business intelligence. The results are loaded into a data warehouse, which also contains data from various shipment, cost, and routing systems.

Once they had all that precious data, they needed a way to get it back to customers for reporting, trend analysis, and carrier negotiations. Enter WebFOCUS. nVision used Information Builders data visualization technology and location analytics to build a dashboard that empowers customers to scrutinize their shipping, payment, and logistics operations. Originally called the iFocus Dashboard, it enables them to view multiple shipping options and make economical choices about their logistics operations. nVision maintains the data and provides these analytical tools via a software-as-a-service (SaaS) environment. Users only need a web browser to manipulate the data to suit their individual needs.

"The information we capture from each transaction increases supply chain visibility and brings verifiable value to our customers' bottom lines," says Luther. "By letting customers access current business intelligence via the web, we deliver greater value by increasing the efficiency and effectiveness of their shipping activities. This application helps these companies save millions of dollars each year."

Up the Ante

Until recently, nVision customers could analyze the data generated during those transactions, but reporting was limited and required extensive staff support. So nVision created an InfoApp to take these analytic services to the next level. Put simply, they wanted to put control in the hands of the user community.

"We wanted to make clients self-sufficient by adding more advanced analytical functionality, better drill-down capabilities, and a more elegant user experience," Luther recalls. "We already had processing metrics and report cards that allow customers to monitor shipping activity. But they were hungry for more visibility into their data."

InfoApps are custom BI applications that enable non-technical users to easily explore data via charts, graphs, reports, data visualizations, and other highly interactive analytic content. Intuitive and visually compelling, they give the business community instant insight into a complex data set.

To populate this particular InfoApp with useful insights, Luther and his team identified dozens of key performance indicators (KPIs) that they knew would appeal to their customer base. Information Builders developed a proof of concept, which showcased data visualization capabilities along with GIS mapping functionality. The seventeen initial KPIs created by the founding team remain the backbone of iFocus Supply Chain Analytics. Today, however, there are more than 100 new KPIs within this InfoApp, and nVision is adding more all the time.

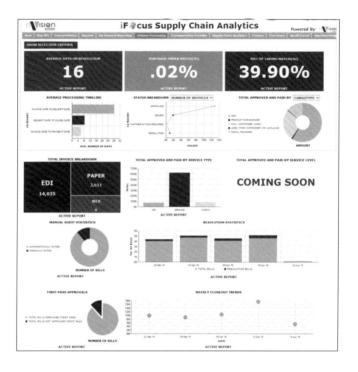

Customers use this interactive BI application to analyze their transportation data. The solution includes global reporting, mapping, graphing, benchmarking, modeling, and network optimization to help them streamline their supply chains. GIS location analytics allow clients to track shipments in transit across all domestic and international locations, then display the data through interactive graphs, gauges, and maps. "Customers love that feature because they can map their lanes from Tokyo to Rotterdam or Tokyo to New York or wherever," Luther explains. "They can see how much activity was in a lane, how many shipments, how much money was involved, how much weight was involved, and so forth."

Users can also create maps based on custom criteria such as service level, origin, destination, division, region, and location. They can slice and dice the information in a variety of ways, and drill down to problem areas to instantly see which shipping lanes need attention.

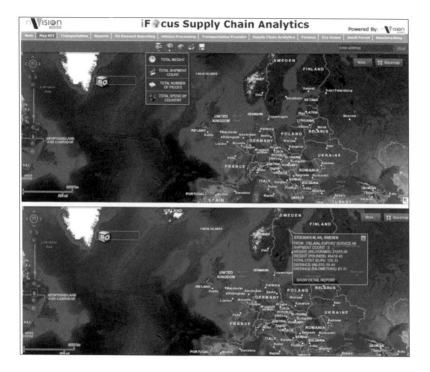

Refine the Analytics

nVision continues to use WebFOCUS to add new capabilities to the InfoApp as well as to create operational and statistical reports for internal users. Current efforts are underway to add customizable tabs, dashboards, and landing pages to meet the needs of different types of users in different operational domains. For example, a finance officer could create a custom page with a dozen financial KPIs. A logistics or business unit operational manager might create a page with departmental KPIs. And so forth.

nVision is also leveraging many years worth of aggregate data to offer benchmarking services. This will allow clients to compare their shipping operations to the shipping operations of other companies, so they can see how they rank against firms of a similar size, industry focus, and location. "That's the advantage of being able to access data from hundreds of customers," Luther notes, "but you can't do things like that without having an analytical tool to present the data."

Before they had WebFOCUS, Luther recalls a benchmarking exercise in which developers had to write more than 300 queries to extract a precise subset of data from the warehouse. Now they can use the InfoApp to instantly get the data and present the visuals. "It's way easier and it has greater impact," he says.

Being able to show transportation providers their precise activity in various lanes and regions gives them better buying power. When they can pull that information together quickly they can negotiate better rates. They can see the top performing lanes as well as the lanes that need attention and then make adjustments to reduce costs and boost efficiency.

For example, a user can click on a digital map to view top-performing lanes within a given time period, including addresses and related bills of lading, then drill down into details like shipment, weight, and distance of travel. These interactive displays allow them to identify cost-reduction strategies.

"In many cases they can reduce costs by switching modes, changing service levels, consolidating shipments, or altering their shipping patterns," Luther explains. "By clicking on hyperlinks they can drill down to individual freight bills and run ad hoc reports to check the status of shipments."

Follow the Dollar

BI applications such as iFocus Supply Chain Analytics fall into the category of Opportunity Capture apps since they are designed to capture new or incremental revenue. They reveal timely business opportunities and allow users to capitalize on them.

In this case approximately 1,500 people depend on the app, including customers and internal users. This type of InfoApp is easy to scale since the entire environment is available as an online service.

According to Luther, nVision's value-added InfoApp saves customers an average of two percent of their annual transportation budget, on top of the five to seven percent that nVision saves them through its traditional auditing services. "There is a measurable value to having clean, harmonized data," he explains. "Our customers can generally save anywhere from three to ten percent, all told. When you're talking about $20 million a year and up in shipping costs, those are pretty big numbers."

In an industry where volume drives pricing, having accurate information about shipping activity helps clients present better proposals, tenders, and RFQs. Better information also leads to better evaluations, which ultimately gets them better contracts. It's no wonder that 95 percent of nVision's new customers use these advanced analytic capabilities. "It's one of the top reasons why clients select us," Luther concludes.

us bank

"Every year, come tax time, we are flooded with requests from customers who want information about their spending histories. We often have to supplement our in-house resources by retaining a third-party service to extract data and mail reports to customers. It gets pretty expensive. Now ScoreBoard will let people access their own data online through a self-service app."

Robert Kaufman
Senior Vice President
U.S. Bank

Financial Services

Chapter Eleven

Helping Customers Analyze Credit Card Purchases

U.S. Bank

Six years ago, U.S. Bank's Payments Solutions division unveiled a new InfoApp called ScoreBoard. At a time when internet banking services were just gaining traction at most large banks, this useful, high-profile service allowed the bank's small business customers to analyze spending patterns on their credit cards, merchant processing accounts, and other types of electronic payment vehicles. It was an instant success. Suddenly, small business owners could compare their corporate spending habits with other companies that have similar industry and geographic profiles. And they could click into interactive dashboards to see customized views of card payment activity, along with one-button access to consolidated statements and reports.

Today U.S. Bank's robust business tool allows millions of clients to monitor corporate spending and easily create reports to analyze data. The customer-facing InfoApp is boosting adoption of U.S. Bank's Internet banking channel, which improves customer loyalty and reduces support costs for the bank. The U.S. Bank team continues to evaluate improvements and changes to the tool to best support its customers.

"ScoreBoard empowers our credit card customers to see spending trends on a monthly, quarterly or annual basis, with the data broken down by market segment," explains Robert Kaufman, senior vice president in the bank's Corporate Payments group and former senior vice president in the Payments Solutions division. "For example, a customer might see that over the last two quarters, 20 percent of their spending went towards travel and entertainment purchases. They can drill down to the individual transactions to analyze their spending. We continue to hear positive feedback about its simplicity. It has been a huge success."

Could they have done it without an app? Kaufman thinks so—but not as easily.

"Previously staff members had to look up this information for customers when they came into the branch or contacted the call center via phone," he explains. "Now, ScoreBoard lets them get the information themselves in a low-cost, low-support environment."

Cutting Costs by Driving Customers to Online Channels

The key driver of an Information Distribution App, like ScoreBoard, is to provide comprehensive documents and information to large numbers of users so they have a complete view of their accounts and business dealings. Information Distribution apps are designed to improve the customer experience and eliminate costs associated with in-person inquiries.

To appeal to its diverse customer base, which includes retailers, restaurants, service bureaus, healthcare companies, and many other types of organizations, U.S. Bank created ScoreBoard in the form of a BI dashboard. It uses colorful graphics to present interactive reports such as the *Merchant Summary*, which offers details about spending at specific merchants. Business customers can view their data by individual cardholder or on a total company basis.

Meanwhile, the *Merchant Detail* report delivers this same information at the transaction level while the Industry Summary report recaps spending by calendar month, either for each individual business card or on a total company basis. Purchase amounts are organized into merchant categories, so small business customers can see exactly where they are spending their money. They can view these reports on the screen, output them to PDF files, or download the data into Microsoft Excel or into Intuit QuickBooks—a huge timesaver for the bank's business customers.

"Of all the technology projects I have been involved with in my career, this has been one of the simplest. I remember thinking, let's build this quickly and inexpensively, and then later we can develop something bigger and better. Well, here we are six years later and it's still being heavily used."

Kaufman credits Information Builders Professional Services for managing a complex project that included several distinct teams from U.S. Bank and its Elavon subsidiary. Business leaders and technologists contributed insight, with help from the U.S. Bank infrastructure team (which hosts the application) and core technology group (which supplies the data).

"We went from idea to implementation in about five months," he recalls. "Of all the technology projects I have been involved with in my career, this has been one of the simplest. I remember thinking, let's build this quickly and inexpensively, and then later we can develop something bigger and better. Well, here we are six years later and it's still being heavily used. We didn't have to rebuild it. People enjoy the value it provides now just as much as they did six years ago."

Simplicity is often the nature of InfoApps. The idea is to create targeted, domain-specific solutions to particular business problems. "My advice is, don't try to boil the ocean," Kaufman adds. "Get it done, get feedback from users, and then move on to the next one."

Which is exactly what U.S. Bank has done.

Buoyed by the success of the first ScoreBoard initiative, the bank recently released a new version of ScoreBoard for its consumer banking customers—six million of them in all. Like the popular small business version, the consumer version of ScoreBoard helps people make smarter decisions about their personal finances. It also provides trending and reporting data so customers can monitor and compare their credit card spending to general consumer trends.

Consumer ScoreBoard includes three useful reports. The *Merchant Summary* reveals where customers are spending their money. The *Industry Summary* groups their purchases by specific categories, such as Gas or Travel or Groceries. The *Annual Summary* allows them to view a full year's worth of data, both in summary and detailed views. U.S. Bank cardholders can also use the free application to download their own reports in HTML, Excel or PDF formats. It is available to all U.S. Bank cardholders who have credit cards, debit cards, and credit lines through U.S. Bank. The reports feature easy-to-read charts and graphs that provide a monthly snapshot of credit-card purchases and payments, such as travel, home improvement and gas purchases.

More Than Just a Pretty Face
InfoApps often appear simple, but looks can be deceiving. It's not just what you see on the front-end that make these apps useful, but what they do behind the scenes to ensure a scalable, high-performance experience. With 6 million potential users—800,000 of who use ScoreBoard regularly—the information architects had to ensure that the system could perform.

U.S. Bank selected WebFOCUS to create its customer-facing InfoApps not only because it can create compelling applications quickly, but also because it has a robust back-end architecture that is capable of supporting large numbers of users with minimal infrastructure. Its server-based reporting architecture provides a foundation for large-scale deployments at a relatively low cost. Built-in load-balancing and failover processes distribute the load across multiple back-end servers. Native data-adapters speed up information retrieval, while a sophisticated data manipulation engine generates complex reports in one or two passes through the database. WebFOCUS queries are dynamically partitioned, with complex number crunching and aggregation operations optimized across the back-end database and reporting servers, not on Web servers or front-end devices. Thus a single processor can serve multiple, simultaneous user requests, maximizing system performance.

U.S. Bank's system administrators can easily scale-out each tier of this clustered architecture by using Information Builders' Cluster Load Management software, Autonomic Server, and Workload Distribution Facility, which intelligently route requests to servers with the most available capacity. Information Builders also developed a custom security module to seamlessly integrate ScoreBoard with U.S. Bank's existing Merchant Dashboard environment via a single sign-on process.

A Huge Return on Invested Capital
Technically, it's impressive, but Kaufman prefers to focus on the business benefits. He says unique offerings such as ScoreBoard help U.S. Bank attract new clients and retain

existing ones, driving revenue and building long-term value for the company. He foresees big savings in the call center, especially as the Consumer ScoreBoard gains traction.

"Every year, come tax time, we are flooded with requests from customers who want information about their spending histories. We often have to supplement our in-house resources by retaining a third-party service to extract data and mail reports to customers. It gets pretty expensive. Now ScoreBoard will let people access their own data online through a self-service app."

Whether it's a business that wants to know the split between supplies, utilities and repairs, or a consumer who wants to know the difference between going out to eat and paying their utility bill, the demand for data is always there. Prior to ScoreBoard, U.S. Bank had no easy way to give customers this information.

ScoreBoard has been providing value for many years, with very little ongoing investment. According to Kaufman, U.S. Bank spent about a quarter of a million dollars to get the first InfoApp online, yet it has easily saved the company tens of millions of dollars so far. One way to quantify those savings is to calculate the immense expense involved in training thousands of customer-facing employees to supply credit card information to customers—not to mention staffing up the call centers and branches during busy times of the year.

"The cost savings have been substantial and there has been a significant payback," he confirms. "With internet banking services like ScoreBoard, fewer people contact the call center and fewer people visit the branches, which has a direct impact on costs. The bang for the buck with an investment like this, versus the investment we were making to improve physical interactions with customers, is like night and day."

"As you look at SnackBoard, one question leads to another question, which leads to another question, and so on. You don't always know where these questions will take you next. That's the power of this app. You don't have to sift through reports or hope a report exists to find the answers you need."

Steve Toth
Chief Information Officer
Utz Quality Foods

Snack Food Manufacturing

Chapter Twelve

Optimizing Inventory, Sales, and Production Processes

Utz Quality Foods

Utz Quality Foods, Inc. got its start in 1921 when William and Salie Utz scraped together $300 to launch Hanover Home Brand Potato Chips in a small-town kitchen in Hanover, Pennsylvania. Back then, cooking 50 pounds of chips per hour was an accomplishment and the first section of the Utz plant was built behind William and Salie's home. The start-up company sold fresh chips to small local grocers and markets in and around South Central Pennsylvania and Baltimore, Maryland.

Fast-forward 95 years. Today Utz Quality Foods, Inc. has six manufacturing facilities in Pennsylvania and additional facilities in Louisiana, California, Colorado, and Massachusetts—10 facilities in all in addition to sixty-plus distribution centers throughout the east coast of the United States. Utz is now the largest independent, privately held snack brand in the United States, producing over 3.6 million pounds of snacks per week while operating over 1100 distribution routes. The snack food producer now sells chips in 395 different flavors and iterations, including Crab Potato Chips and Yuengling BBQ Potato Chips. Last year, Utz produced 175 million pounds of snacks and brought in over $600 million in revenue.

One of the keys to Utz's steady growth has been its ability to effectively service the stores that sell its products. Success is a byproduct not only of fresh, high-quality products, but fresh information.

Utz started to embrace analytics nearly 15 years ago when the senior management team realized they needed up-to-the-minute insight to efficiently service customers—which include small mom and pop grocers as well as some of the world's largest retailers.

"There's a transformational shift going on at Utz," explains Steve Toth, the company's Chief Information Officer. "We want to be more data-driven as we measure not only what we have done in the past, but where we are going in the future. We are beginning to use more analytic tools to make better, more forward-looking decisions."

Steve joined Utz two years ago to fill the role of CIO due to his extensive experience developing strategies and leading teams, as well as his solid background with corporate acquisitions. He has worked in multiple industries, from small internet startups with $15 million in sales to international conglomerates that turn over $9 billion. Prior to joining Utz he was president of sales for a German industrial company. He has also led marketing teams, project management organizations, and shared service organizations. He is currently working to transform Utz's IT department from a report-writing organization into a value-driven support organization that helps the business units become self-sufficient. "Right now we are a report-driven organization, which gives us a static view of the past," he explains. "We want to speed up the decision-making cycle and change the value model as we empower our business units to take control of and unlock their own information."

To achieve this vision, Utz used WebFOCUS to create an InfoApp branded SnackBoard that provides employees fast and clear answers to business questions related to sales, manufacturing, and finance. People throughout the company use SnackBoard to drill into sales data via charts, graphs, reports, data visualizations, and other interactive methods. Utz is in the process of preparing similar InfoApps for finance, manufacturing, and executive-level decision-making.

A Recipe For Success
Utz uses a direct store delivery (DSD) model to deliver its goods to major accounts such as Safeway, Kroger, Wal-Mart, BJ's and Target. DSD is a popular sales and distribution method in the food industry, where keeping fresh products on store shelves means minimizing the number of days in the supply chain. Utz handles most

of its distribution via its own network to get its pretzels, chips, and other snacks from the ovens to the shelves as quickly as possible.

Bypassing distribution centers owned by third parties and distributing goods directly to the point of consumption certainly makes economic sense—not to mention ensuring the freshest possible products for consumers. But the onus is on Utz to carefully monitor in-store inventory and maintain relationships with retailers. SnackBoard allows Utz regional sales managers to monitor the operation and determine how well they are meeting sales goals by examining data through nine views or widgets including sales goals, warehouse goals, labor, and stale & damaged goods. All of the data is easily sorted by category, brand, customer, and channel.

"This is information that the sales team needs every day to gauge the health of our key accounts," Steve says. "By monitoring these nine metrics they always know where they stand in relation to their goals. They can drill down to view year-over-year comparisons from the company level all the way down to an individual route sales professional level, and even down to the actual SKU items."

Steve refers to this type of analysis as conversational management. Each user has the flexibility to follow whatever path of inquiry he or she wants to pursue. "As you look at SnackBoard, one question leads to another question, which leads to another question, and so on," he explains. "You don't always know where these questions will take you next. That's the power of this app. You don't have to sift through reports or hope a report exists to find the answers you need."

Spicing Up Sales

The Utz business community uses the phrase "blocking top and bottom" to describe this type of analysis. For example, a manager examining sales in a particular channel might examine the bottom 10 accounts to figure out how to move them up the ranks. Or he might look at the top 10 accounts to figure out what is working, so he can apply their best practices to the others. One day, the focus might be on improving margins. The next day it might be on manufacturing capacity. "If we have more manufacturing capacity than we need, we might not worry so much about margins and instead concentrate on pushing sales. This app allows us to nimbly react to the daily business conditions."

Steve still remembers the excitement that seized the 12-person operating team the first time he showed them how to use SnackBoard to select, qualify, sort, and summarize sales data. While the team had previously given Steve the go-ahead to proceed with the development of SnackBoard, none of them knew what to expect until he gave them a sneak peak at this early version.

"I was demonstrating the prototype to four executive vice presidents, and they all wanted to get SnackBoard into production immediately," he recalls. "The value of such a tool was clearly evident because it delivered capabilities that did not exist." For example, one member of the operating team suggested that they could do away with their monthly team meetings, since there would be less reason to get together just to share information. Another said they could use SnackBoard to diagnose problems and resolve them immediately, as opposed to waiting until the end of the month or the end of the quarter.

What began as a five-minute presentation turned into a 40-minute demonstration as Steve put SnackBoard through its paces. "The conversation evolved from WHAT was being presented to HOW to unlock the information to truly analyze the data," he adds. "The excitement was evident and they naturally dove right in. The mechanics of using the app did not matter as much as their desire to derive insights from it."

A Taste of Things to Come

Utz's success with SnackBoard is just one of the company's many successes with business intelligence technology. Their story mimics the evolution of the BI industry, from simple reporting to complex data visualization to interactive analytics to business unit self-sufficiency. SnackBoard is the latest iteration of a well-construed BI strategy that is extending analytic capabilities throughout the organization.

Their use of BI has also matched the growth of the company—both its steady revenue growth as well as its expansion by acquisition. In 2011, Utz purchased the "Dirty" and Zapp's brands of potato chips, responding to the same "craft" trend that altered the beer market and continues to make waves in the snack food industry. "People want products that are interesting," Utz CEO Dylan Lissette told Fortune in

2015, adding that they had a similar motivation for purchasing Bachman in 2012 and the Good Health brand in 2014, which helped Utz to gain relevance in the fast moving "good-for-you" category.

For all of these brands, one of the central motivating factors behind Utz's corporate progression is to drive closer and closer to a just-in-time operation. In the snack food industry, timing is a crucial element in keeping fresh product on store shelves. That's why Utz uses WebFOCUS dashboards to coordinate activities among its production, marketing, sales, and distribution operations. Its BI environment delivers daily sales breakdowns—product-by-product and store-by-store—in a form that is easy for busy salespeople to digest.

Another important InfoApp is called UtzFOCUS, a dashboard that allows Route Sales Professionals (RSPs) to analyze sales and distribution information as they carry out their routes. The data that they enter as they make their rounds improves visibility throughout the supply chain. Regional managers use UtzFOCUS to determine how much of a certain product is selling on a given day, how much product was sold into a particular store or chain, at what price, and in response to what promotions. If they determine that the sales team is not properly servicing a store, they can find the source of the problem and correct it quickly.

In addition, Utz conducts vendor-managed inventory (VMI) with some of its retailers, which means the RSPs are responsible for properly servicing accounts with the appropriate levels of inventory and variety on the store shelves. VMI is popular in the retail and CPG industries due to its ability to smooth demand and increase sales by tying daily production and shipments to actual needs. As Utz has learned, VMI programs are most successful when suppliers can exchange real-time information about promotions and inventory levels with their retailers.

In Utz's case, the RSPs who sell products to the stores collect data using mobile devices. These personnel use UtzFOCUS to execute dozens of transactions, including buying back product that is no longer fresh and selling new product into the store. RSPs record daily inventory information as they make their rounds from store to store.

Each day a central database is updated with this current inventory and demand information from all of the salespeople. WebFOCUS crunches through the data to make it available for self-service reporting. Utz serves over 66,000 individual stores on a weekly basis.

Regional managers use the BI environment to make daily decisions about inventory, sales, and trends. For example, they might compare last week's sales results to the results from the same week a year earlier, drilling down to isolate areas of interest. WebFOCUS also helps them root out problems, such as when sales are lagging in a particular region or store.

Tying daily production more closely to sales also enables the company to streamline its supply of products and other supplies, so the factories maintain just enough inventories for current needs. If Utz decides to discount a product for a promotion in an account, RSPs can review the current inventory, then solicit store managers for special placement on the shelves, as well as for off-shelve promotional displays, based on their instant analysis of how a similar promotion boosted sales in the past. Users can run reports, apply filters or calculations, and visualize data with a few clicks or taps.

"If you don't measure you can't improve," Steve concludes. "We are implementing quite a few metrics and elevating some of them to key performance indicators [KPIs] that allow managers to measure progress against goals. That, to me, is operational excellence."

LUTHERAN LIFE
COMMUNITIES

"Employees across our six campuses feel more like they are part of a bigger picture. They can learn from each other and help each other. All managers can see best practices so they know what is working at each site."

Roger W. Paulsberg
President and Chief Executive Officer
Lutheran Life Communities

Senior Living Facilities

Chapter Thirteen

Lutheran Life Communities Creates InfoApp to Improve
Operational Performance

Lutheran Life Communities

For more than 120 years, Lutheran Life Communities has been recognized as one of America's finest senior living communities. Established in 1892 as The Altenheim in Arlington Heights, Illinois, the nonprofit organization now comprises six continuing care retirement communities serving thousands of people across Illinois, Indiana, and Florida.

While rapid growth in recent years has delivered numerous benefits to community residents, it has also introduced administrative challenges for organization leaders. Operational data was spread across seven information systems, making it difficult for directors and department heads to put their hands on the information they needed to support day-to-day decision-making. Roger W. Paulsberg, president and CEO of Lutheran Life Communities, sought a business analytics solution that could consolidate information about daily operations and present insights to managers, directors, and executives in an actionable way.

Roger describes the company's previous data gathering processes as "convoluted and difficult." For example, census data that represents residential occupancy levels and payment categories was collected manually, input into Excel spreadsheets, and e-mailed to stakeholders. Labor and productivity data was isolated in payroll systems. Important benchmarks, including metrics about food and dining, were only created when requested. Automated processes were scarce, and information distribution was slow.

Lutheran Life Communities' senior officers knew it was time to deploy a more modern information platform, but they didn't want just another reporting system.

"We had a vision for a business intelligence system that would raise performance tracking to a new level," Roger explains. "We quickly recognized the customizability and flexibility of the WebFOCUS technology. We could build a user-friendly analytic environment and run it ourselves, adding new functionality to suit the changing needs of our business, such as interactive dashboards with overlays that depict where our revenue comes from."

A Better Way to Collect and Share Information

Continuing care retirement communities, also known as life plan communities, are senior living campuses that offer a full continuum of care. For example, in the Independent Living options on a campus, residents can occupy an apartment or villa as healthy, independent individuals. If they need more care they can move to Assisted Living, where more meals are provided and residents can receive help with medicines and basic services. Skilled Nursing care, both short-term and residential, as well as memory supportive living, is also available, if and when residents need it.

To monitor the many moving parts of this cost-sensitive business, Lutheran Life Communities created an InfoApp called Shipshape that extends budgetary responsibility throughout the organization. It takes results from many information systems and distills a large volume of data into an actionable format. Instead of being overwhelmed by intensive reporting and data management tasks, business users can see relevant information at a glance. Comparative metrics enable benchmarking among all departments and campuses and allow managers to assess the relative performance of the activities under their purview.

At the outset of the project, Lutheran Life Communities worked with Information Builders and RDC Business Solutions to define operational metrics related to census, labor, revenue, and dining. Nurse managers at the residential communities gather census data each night. In addition, daily labor and productivity data is collected from the Empower timecard system and financial results are imported from the general ledger. Other operational statistics come from the ERP system.

WebFOCUS analytic templates made it easy to define KPIs and embed them into interactive displays. All metrics are standardized so that senior managers can oversee the operation in a consistent way. Each KPI provides a high-level snapshot of the measures that are important to that business unit. Managers define the target performance levels and establish budgets; WebFOCUS displays progress through dashboards that contain interactive graphs, making it easy to see variances from stated targets.

According to Steve Duchene, corporate director of facilities at Lutheran Life Communities, Shipshape provides a convenient way to interact with operational data by supplying a constant readout on the organization's performance in key cost areas. It allows the people responsible for those areas to compare actual expenditures against budgets so they don't stray too far from their goals.

As the person responsible for plant operations, maintenance, grounds keeping, security, housekeeping, laundry, capital projects, and construction, Steve says that in addition to boosting knowledge, Shipshape boosts camaraderie. "Employees across our six campuses feel more like they are part of a bigger picture," he explains. "They can learn from each other and help each other. All managers can see best practices so they know what is working at each site."

Unlike a static reporting system, which simply produces summaries of past activity, this InfoApp empowers business users to explore the data via charts, graphs, and other interactive content. The goal is to influence organizational behavior and encourage standout performance by allowing managers to monitor day-to-day metrics that pertain to their exact areas of the business. Encouraging accountability allows everyone to learn from each other as they assess net differences among campuses.

The system makes it easy for employees to obtain insights on their own. It flattens the hierarchy and empowers managers to see trends in the data. By transforming a large and diverse data set into actionable data points, they can see how their portion of the business is trending, then drill down to follow unique paths of inquiry.

For example, a bar chart that displays food costs identifies communities that have exceeded their allotted budgets in red, while those that are at or under budget are displayed in green. Users can choose parameters and drill into these displays to see specific details. Other bar charts reveal budgeted versus actual food costs, as shown in the following image.

The InfoApp tracks expenditures against budgets according to user-defined increments, such as one month, six months, and year-to-date. Color-coded displays allow managers to assess strengths, weaknesses, and possible areas for improvement. Financial metrics such as labor hours per patient per day are compared against budgets, which are carefully set up at the start of each year. The metrics are displayed as KPIs that keep everyone from finance officers to nurse-managers apprised of important developments within their purview (see the following image).

"Whether it's for raw food costs, caregiver hours per patient day, or any other number of variables, there is a comparison of how well each area and each campus is doing against their assumptions on a daily basis," says Roger. "If a department or community strays too far from its budgetary goals, then a senior management colleague can step in to help. Everybody sees what I see because we have a unified view of the business. Data from all our major business areas is represented in a standardized way, and much of it is updated daily. With a couple of clicks you can go from the entire corporation to

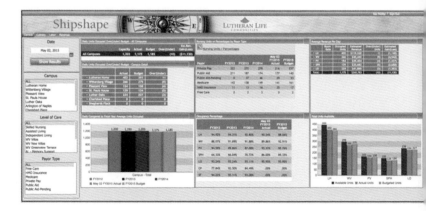

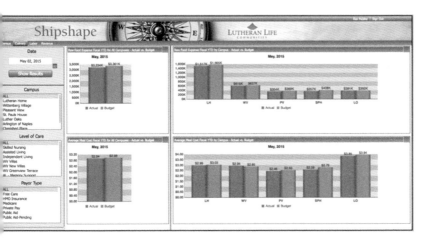

a particular department at a particular campus, then down to a particular metric, such as a particular site's culinary costs per meal," he adds.

The dashboards also highlight the highest expense areas in the highest revenue-generating areas, helping Lutheran Life Communities maximize its $100 million annual budget. For example, culinary metrics tell food service managers how much it costs to feed one resident for each meal based on all the associated labor costs, food costs, and so forth. If culinary costs are too low at a particular campus, perhaps its dining establishments need to improve meal quality. If they are too high they might need to be more judicious in the menu selections. "Our dietary managers and culinary managers watch these metrics very closely," Roger says. "If there is an anomaly we can jump on it right away. We don't have to wait to receive a report."

Population data is another good example. Continuing care communities must maintain an optimum case mix, which refers to the ratio of public-aid residents versus self-funded residents. Lutheran Life Communities wants to fill all the beds but there are limits to how many public aid residents they are licensed for and can afford, which means they must keep a close eye on the case mix of subsidized versus private-pay residents.

"It comes back to good stewardship of the dollars that are entrusted to us," says Roger. "The phrase we use is, 'No margin, no mission.' This InfoApp helps administrators and managers monitor our census metrics. The variables change so quickly, which is why we needed a way to standardize and share information among a broadly dispersed team."

Performance Data Drives Accountability

InfoApps like Shipshape are often called performance or accountability apps because they extend responsibility throughout the organization. The main objective of a performance/accountability app is to keep specific activities on track. InfoApps not only provide daily feedback on departmental performance. They also enable users to examine the data. People don't have to rely on hunches. They can see what works and why, department-to-department and campus-to-campus—every day.

Before Shipshape came on the scene, managers at each Lutheran Life Community sometimes felt isolated and cut off from the activities at other sites. On average, managers scrutinized important metrics only once each month. "The information might have been three weeks old by the time anyone could see it, and by then it wasn't particularly relevant," says Steve. "Now we look at current data every day."

Most managers understand the value of formalizing performance-management processes, but previously they were hindered by rigid data-management and analytic tools. These limitations made it difficult to align strategies and goals with day-to-day initiatives—and to promote behavior that leads to improved performance. Waiting until after the close of each accounting period is too late to have a decisive impact on costs. Now managers can examine leading indicators through dashboards that always reflect the current state of the operation, as well as drill down to detailed operational, quality, and service measures as specific activities occur.

The analytic environment greets users whenever they access the corporate intranet. For example, every day the director of nursing at each site examines staffing levels—

"Everybody sees what I see because we have a unified view of the business. Data from all our major business areas is represented in a standardized way, and much of it is updated daily."

not only to gauge financial performance, but for regulatory reasons as well since the health department requires Lutheran Life Communities to maintain certain staffing levels.

"There is a sweet spot between sparing no expense in providing the very best care and meeting minimum requirements," Roger notes. "We want to ensure patient satisfaction and clinical excellence while making good use of funds. If this type of metric is off for a few days it can put a budget behind for quite some time. That's why it's important to make corrections quickly so campuses don't churn through a month's budget in two or three weeks. The InfoApp tells them if something is not right or the business is not on course. This knowledge allows us to make adjustments before such adjustments become painful."

The InfoApp is accessed by corporate directors in charge of each area of the business, executive directors at six locations, regional financial controllers, and department heads for nursing care, marketing, and other divisions. Comparative metrics enable benchmarking among all departments and campuses. Each user can see the relative performance of the activities under his or her purview. Being able to see organization-wide numbers helps everyone appreciate the impact of their activities on the business as a whole.

"Users like the speed with which they can get the information they need," Duchene says. "WebFOCUS has exceeded our expectations."

Boosting Efficiency Throughout the System

There is no question that WebFOCUS has delivered measurable benefits to Lutheran Life Communities. For example, it helps managers in the dining and culinary department adjust food orders to meet fluctuating demand. Being able to accurately calculate the amount of food that is required at each community reduces waste, boosts meal quality, and improves the bottom line.

Labor and benefits, which represent 55 percent of the business, are now managed more effectively because managers no longer need to wait until the end of a longer time period to get information. Being able to see the daily metrics helps them to set short- and long-term goals—and then monitor performance to attain those goals.

"Now that data is driving the business, we can more accurately match staff levels to the number of residents," Roger says. "Managing volatility benefits everybody over the long run."

Roger agrees. "Information Builders is a great partner with great technology," he concludes. "They helped us deploy an intuitive, automated system that fits our budget. It's a vast improvement over our old methods of gathering and sharing information. We're very happy with the way it turned out."

ⓦ iovation®

"Our solution runs in the background. It's completely automatic, so customers can't always see exactly what it's doing. Now we can run reports that show them just how many times business rules were invoked, or how many suspicious transactions were flagged for further investigation or blocked completely. The analytics make it very clear how we are keeping their sites protected."

Greg Pierson
Chief Executive Officer
iovation

Fraud Prevention

Chapter Fourteen

Battling Internet Fraud With Analytics

iovation

iovation was founded in 2004 with one simple goal—to make the Internet a safer place for people to do business and interact. The Portland, Oregon-based company protects online businesses and their customers against fraud and abuse. It also identifies trustworthy customers through a combination of advanced technologies such as device identification, shared device reputation, device-based authentication, and real-time risk evaluation.

To provide its clients with greater visibility into fraudulent activities and to differentiate itself from competitors, iovation bolstered its Fraud Prevention solution with BI technology from Information Builders. Fraud management teams, both internally and at its client sites, use WebFOCUS InfoApps to investigate transaction details, device histories, and suspicious visitors.

iovation's analytic technology not only gives customers and support staff access to intelligence they didn't previously have, but also enables iovation to monetize its data by expanding and reinforcing the benefits it provides to its clients. Customers use WebFOCUS to closely monitor system activity. Insight from the InfoApps reveal exactly how iovation's Fraud Prevention solution protects them.

Mitigating Fraud, Minimizing Loss

The rise of the digital economy has made business intelligence applications for eliminating loss, waste, and abuse essential. Keep in mind that "loss prevention" is much bigger than just online commerce and online transactions. Losses occur for many reasons and analytic applications can often reveal the causes. For example, retailers consider merchandise that does not sell well to represent a loss. Proper marketing, better exposure, and employee training can help reduce these losses—with analytics as the guide. Every industry and every sector must battle loss in some form, and analytic technology can help.

According to Kurk Spendlove, director of engineering at iovation, the key to effectively combating fraud is to remain one step ahead of fraudsters by proactively detecting and blocking suspicious transactions before they are executed. It's a huge growth market for analytics. Risk mitigation, fraud detection, and loss prevention are round-the-clock activities at nearly every large enterprise that does business online.

In this case, more than 3,500 fraud managers in retail, financial services, insurance, social networking, gaming, and other industries leverage iovation's database of information about billions of Internet devices to determine the level of risk associated with online transactions. This database, and iovation's associated information systems, run around the clock to protect 16 million transactions and stop an average of 300,000 fraudulent activities every day.

An Organization Driven by Technology

iovation has its roots in the online gaming arena. As time went by, senior officers realized that the fraud prevention technology that they had created to protect their gaming apps was unique. This technology soon became iovation's mainline, and since then these security products have spread rapidly—not only in the online gaming industry, but in many other commercial sectors as well. "The light bulb went off when we realized that many of our clients were more interested in the support tools that we built for ourselves than they were in the online gaming platform that we were offering," Kurk recalls.

A new business model was born but it was dependent on analytics to succeed. iovation's secret sauce is what Kurk calls an "association matrix" that reveals connections among related accounts and devices. It's a bit like Facebook, with its nested associations of friends, friends-of-friends, and so forth. But in this case the associations are applied to devices and accounts rather than to people.

For example, you might use a MacBook Pro® at work, a Dell® PC at home, an iPad® when you travel, and an iPhone® throughout the day. If you normally use your PC to login to your banking app, and you suddenly login with your iPad, iovation can tell that it is a related device due to its common user profiles and account activities. Within this continuously expanding web, iovation uses analytics to develop a progressively greater understanding of the vast network of anonymous consumers that reside behind millions of seemingly unrelated transactions.

iovation has built a knowledge base that contains information about the physical devices used to conduct online transactions. It calculates a "reputation" for each device based on previous fraud history, associations with other bad accounts or devices, and real-time risk assessments. Clients are alerted if a device directly or indirectly associated with a known fraudster tries to access one of their sites. For example, if a user commits fraud on a financial site using an iPhone, then taps over to a retail site using that same phone, iovation will alert the retailer of potential malicious intentions, even if it is that user's first visit.

"Taking a device-based view allows us to extend intelligence cross customer boundaries via our consortium," Kurk says. "We expose our clients to risk profiles that they would otherwise never see. For example, an internet user might move from a retail site to a financial site to a dating site to a social network site. By looking at the transactions that are executed by that user's device, we can tie all those things together."

iovation's clients often conduct in-depth forensic research to gain visibility into fraudulent actions and trends. That's where WebFOCUS business intelligence comes in. Interactive reports and InfoApps allow clients to analyze actual and potential threats. They can run complete transaction histories, or keep track of the number of suspicious transactions over time to figure out when peaks occur. For example, they might want to obtain information about a specific device from a third party. WebFOCUS analytics let them investigate further—and to determine how that device has interacted with their site in the past.

A New Portal, with Analytics at its Core

iovation created an analytic portal that contains several InfoApps and more than 100 reports, in addition to reports that are generated on a nightly basis and sent out to approximately 450 customers. These reports allow clients to see how their transactions are trending over time. For example, they might see that yesterday they were denying two percent of total transactions and today they are denying four percent. Interactive pie charts reveal the percentage of traffic that comes from the U.S. versus outside the U.S., broken out by country, along with lots of device metrics.

"A client might ask, 'What percentage of my transactions are coming through on Windows devices versus iPhones or iPads?'" Kurk suggests. "Users can plug in parameters to select different groupings of customers, such as retail businesses or gambling businesses or financial businesses."

iovation's internal customer support team is more productive thanks to its ability to access the new analytic portal. Team members use the portal to analyze information contained in the knowledge base. This allows them to instantly answer complex questions and share insights gleaned from other customers.

"When we put more information in the hands of our customers, we minimize the number of calls placed to our support staff," states Greg Pierson, CEO at iovation. "But they still frequently receive inquiries from customers with more complicated questions."

For example, some clients use the InfoApps to determine what percentage of their traffic comes from a certain type of device. Others use InfoApps to learn about best practices that other clients have implemented to combat fraud. In addition, the analytic portal helps iovation convey the value of its solutions to its customers. "Our solution runs in the background," Greg says. "It's completely automatic, so customers can't always see exactly what it's doing. Now we can run reports that show them just how many times business rules were invoked, or how many suspicious transactions were flagged for further investigation or blocked completely. The analytics make it very clear how we are keeping their sites protected."

THE MANUFACTURING CLOUD

"Our customers demanded a world-class BI platform to gain insights into all of the data they generate in the Plex Manufacturing Cloud. Most of these customers want a drag-and-drop experience. They don't want to have to join tables together to create reports, or even need to understand the underlying data architecture. IntelliPlex makes that possible. It is easy to join data sources in a logical manner, which eliminates the adoption barrier for customers."

Matt Young
Senior Technical Engineer
Plex Systems

Cloud Computing

Chapter Fifteen

Ruling the Cloud With Embedded Analytics

Plex Systems

In 2001, Plex Systems established itself as one of the first software vendors to understand the power and potential of the cloud. Delivering Plex as a service made it possible to deliver solutions for manufacturers that typically face tight cost constraints and run lean IT operations, opening up an opportunity to disrupt legacy enterprise resource planning (ERP) and manufacturing execution systems (MES).

It was a prescient move. Plex has built a fast growing, profitable business by focusing on the needs of manufacturers—and by creating a unique and cost-effective cloud strategy. Today the Plex Manufacturing Cloud delivers industry-leading ERP and MES functionality to more than 500 companies across the process manufacturing and discrete manufacturing sectors.

Plex partnered with Information Builders to embed a customizable analytic environment within the Plex Manufacturing Cloud, replacing a costly and cumbersome legacy reporting environment. Branded "IntelliPlex," the analytic environment provides a set of Web-based design tools that let business users drag and drop data elements into custom reports, dashboards, and analytic applications. Based on WebFOCUS and InfoAssist, IntelliPlex helps manufacturers understand every aspect of their businesses.

Plex has spread analytic capabilities to thousands of people by encouraging two basic categories of users: IntelliPlex *builders*, who create reports, charts, scorecards, and dashboards; and IntelliPlex *users*, who consume these BI assets. According to Matt Young, senior technical engineer at Plex Systems, the IntelliPlex business intelligence

(BI) environment is seamlessly included in customers' solutions, leveraging data from the shop floor, suppliers, customers, and dozens of other information sources. Reports are run from simple URLs that can be embedded in any portal or analytic application or menu. IntelliPlex runs in the cloud, giving users all the functionality they need, when and where they need it.

"Our customers demanded a world-class, high-performance BI platform to gain insights into all of the data they generate in the Plex Manufacturing Cloud," Matt explains. "Most of these customers want a drag-and-drop experience. They don't want to have to join tables together to create reports, or even need to understand the underlying data architecture. IntelliPlex makes that possible. It is easy to join data sources in a logical manner, which eliminates the adoption barrier for customers."

Rolling Out Robust and Flexible Analytic Services

Plex Systems has always had a rich information set. However, before they created IntelliPlex, their customers had to create reports in a SQL programming environment. Today a large portion of the Plex customer base uses IntelliPlex to create their own BI environments. In addition, Plex's engineering and product management teams have developed turnkey analytic applications and portals based on their understanding of the enterprise needs of these customers—making it even easier for customers to gain

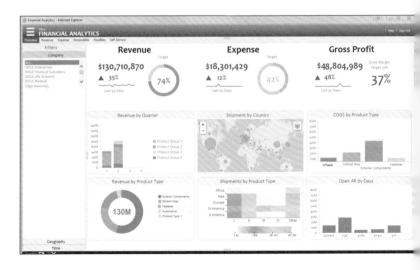

insight into their organizations, and creating a new revenue stream for Plex. Analytic domains and applications cover financials, production, procurement, sales, and other business functions.

"Over the past three years we had two major goals for IntelliPlex: make it easier for customers to access and analyze their data, and deliver that analysis as quickly as possible," Matt continues. "We did this by implementing an analytics data warehouse and developing business views of this data. This made developing and executing reports a breeze for our business analyst users, eliminating the need for IT help."

Matt and his team also developed a series of domain-specific IntelliPlex analytic applications that continue to set Plex apart and drive sales for the company by providing premium content for customers. He says being able to easily share business data in this way has also helped to solidify account relations. He recalls a recent situation when an analyst in the Customer Care department used one of the new analytic applications to visualize annual cost trends for a struggling customer. "The analytic application performed like a dream and the report was so easy to develop," he adds. "We had a mock-up done in about three minutes. Everyone on the call was floored. Tears were literally shed and hugs were exchanged."

Visualizing Data for Manufacturing Customers
The InfoAssist architecture is popular with SaaS vendors because it can be readily embedded into a larger solution or rebranded within a third-party application. Matt calls the Plex integration "seamless" because users only need one set of credentials to access Plex Manufacturing Cloud and its associated analytic environment. They can access rich functionality via computers, tablets, and mobile devices. WebFOCUS supports the multi-tenant architecture upon which Plex is built. And Plex's single-instance deployment model meshes nicely with WebFOCUS.

Within this customized BI environment, nontechnical users can use IntelliPlex to filter information, visualize it through interactive displays, and share it with others. IntelliPlex makes it easy to combine external data with results from Plex tables, standard views, and custom SQL procedures. Users can customize their own reporting environments and leverage a library of standard reports as well.

What do customers do with all this data? The Plex Manufacturing Cloud enables organizations to increase throughput at their manufacturing facilities, understand where they are most exposed to risk, proactively respond to customer demands, and contend with the crushing volume of data emerging from today's plant floors. Unlike general-purpose ERP systems, Plex was built "from the plant floor up" for precisely this purpose.

Many Plex customers define their own KPIs to assist with traceability, which involves finding problems at the source and then taking action to remediate them. For example, if a brake manufacturer learns about a bad shipment of brake pads, quality control managers can use IntelliPlex to trace the serial number of one or more defective parts and then track the associated lots through the manufacturing process to determine where the defect originated. A sales manager could follow the same approach to examine results by region or sector, then drill down to individual invoices to determine which sales people are performing well. Similarly, an inventory manager could use IntelliPlex to keep workers apprised of projected and actual quantities during manufacturing, assembly, and distribution processes.

Traceability is very important in the manufacturing industry, where companies are always looking at ways to improve product performance, and often have to respond to product recalls and accountability issues. The BI environment helps customers to pinpoint problems, maximize profitability, and extend best practices from department to department, region to region, and even out to supply chain partners.

Each BI portal includes a tab for ad hoc reporting. Users can pick fields, measures, and dimensions, and then click "go" to visualize the data through their own reports. Often it is a progressive progress. For example, if an InfoApp reveals that a certain customer doesn't pay invoices on time, a purchasing manager can create a custom report that lists outstanding invoices.

Keeping a Handle on Manufacturing Operations

IntelliPlex stands out in analyzing operational metrics. A typical mid-size manufacturer might have hundreds of machines working around the clock. Assembly lines generate information that can be used for configuration, troubleshooting, quality control, and maintenance purposes. Each machine captures an immense volume of data at each stage of the manufacturing process. Businesses need manufacturing intelligence to improve quality and traceability, and keep their operations running at peak capacity.

For example, in the production domain, a KPI called operational equipment effectiveness (OEE) helps production personnel keep track of the performance of machines on the plant floor. Most manufacturers use this KPI to monitor when machines are down or offline. However, for a large enterprise, this type of report can take hours to run. Using IntelliPlex and data from the shop floor, Plex can trend OEE for an entire plant over a period of months or even years—in seconds. Users can drill into hot spots on a heat map to study areas of concern, such as plants that are performing at a sub-optimal level or a supply chain problem at a work center within a particular plant. This type of analysis was previously only available to the world's largest manufacturing operations, and these companies had to rely on extensive custom software systems and huge IT staff.

"Line of business users can walk around with their tablets to see how their equipment is performing," says Matt. "They can view pertinent metrics related to number of defects, unexpected levels of downtime, anticipated maintenance, and other variables."

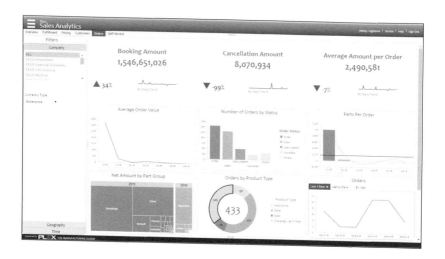

Meanwhile, workers in the purchasing department use IntelliPlex to monitor supplier responsiveness and on-time delivery performance. Graphical reports tell them not only how many parts they are producing moment to moment, but also reveal how production is trending across machines, plants, and the entire enterprise "Previously those reports were difficult to produce," Matt adds. "Now IntelliPlex makes it easy to monitor these trends. We are constantly encouraging our customers to think of their data in a graphical way. It is so much easier to pick out details when the visualizations are done correctly."

The Power of Predictive Analytics

Many Plex customers use Internet of Things (IoT) technologies to collect real-time data from shop floor devices and assembly lines. Plex plans to use this data from the shop floor for predictive analytics. Customers can then use IntelliPlex to assess the performance of systems and equipment, and react to problems before they occur.

For example, consider a machine on the edge of an assembly line that is positioned right in front of a window. During certain hours of the day, sunlight raises the temperature of the machine above the specified operating conditions. This causes an inordinately high number of components to be rejected because they fail a final quality test. It would be easy to use IntelliPlex to evaluate the data stream from this machine and the surrounding environment. An operator might note a temperature fluctuation near the windows versus other parts of the room, and react to this situation as it develops.

In some cases these types of predictive scenarios can be structured as a two-phase process: an auto alert might shut down the machine before it causes a problem with the manufacturing process. Later that day, an operator can analyze the historical data to assess the impact of temperature fluctuations—perhaps adjusting the production schedule or moving the machine to another location further from the window.

Pervasive Insight – From Shop Floor to Top Floor

Many organizations now see the wisdom in moving software functionality off-premises and into the cloud, where it can be operated by technology experts. Plex was one of the first companies to recognize the power of the cloud model. Matt says the "ah ha moment" came early in the company's history as they wrestled with some of their initial customer engagements. "We realized how difficult it was to install, configure, and integrate on-premises software—and how much more efficient it would be to create a multi-tenant application that could be accessed and shared through the cloud," he recalls. "We were investing a lot of time going to customer sites, setting up their servers, and maintaining their ERP systems. We wanted to provide an easier experience for our customers."

By making the software available in the cloud and delivering functionality as a set of services, customers would be relieved of the burden of owning, operating, and maintaining a critical software application and the associated infrastructure. "They would be able to enjoy new features as they became available, yet not have to install, upgrade, or maintain new versions," Matt adds. "Everybody would be on one code base, and we would maintain it for them."

Today such cloud strategies are common, especially as the surrounding network and carrier infrastructure steadily improve to allow for scalable, secure, thin-client deployments. Plex was ahead of its time—and now the company finds itself in a sweet spot as the software industry makes a definitive migration to the cloud. Many software vendors are struggling to re-position their products for this type of service model, and the big ERP vendors face an uphill climb retrofitting their wares and operations for the cloud.

Meanwhile, Plex has focused on adding robust technology that sets it apart from the crowd. IntelliPlex remains central to that vision because it helps customers capture near real-time insight about shop floor activities, and even look beyond their own walls to other parts of the supply chain. With ERP data refreshed every few hours, there is lots of information to analyze from this intricate web of interactions. For example, a supplier can log in to the ERP system to note when a product was shipped to a customer, to monitor raw material requirements, or to peruse problem-control records. Sharing data via the embedded BI tools and analytics facilitates collaboration and simplifies problem-solving by making it easier to gauge production activity, track deliveries, monitor shipments, and analyze supply chain activity.

Matt says IntelliPlex is a huge improvement over their previous reporting environment because it removes barriers between users and their data. "Our customers are innovating with IntelliPlex in a way they were never able to do before," he concludes. "I hear stories all the time about how users are building BI experiences into their every-day business practices. Our customers derive lots of value from these analytic tools, and they are defining that value themselves."

vantiv.™

"Since we began analyzing big data, the intelligence equity of our organization has moved into a very different realm. Previously, our ability to extract customer insights was limited. All we could do was access aggregate data. Now we can analyze merchant data at the transaction level to develop more precise pricing models."

Sujit Unni
Senior Leader of Technology
Vantiv

Payment Processing

Chapter Sixteen

Building Trust, Loyalty, and Revenue
Through Payment Analytics

Vantiv

From the world's largest retailers to small mom-and-pop merchants, Vantiv is leading a transformation in the payments industry. The Cincinnati, Ohio-based company offers a variety of payment services through point-of-sales software vendors, financial institutions, value-added resellers, and independent sales organizations.

Vantiv processes more than 23 billion payments each year, which amounts to approximately $842 billion in payment volume. Its innovations include chip-enabled cards, mobile wallets, eCommerce platforms, and payment solutions for businesses of all sizes. Vantiv is also leading the industry with its innovative technology for storing, processing, and analyzing data—lots of it.

"Since we began analyzing big data, the intelligence equity of our organization has moved into a very different realm," says Sujit Unni, senior leader of technology at Vantiv. "Previously, our ability to extract customer insights was limited. All we could do was access aggregate data. Now we can analyze merchant data at the transaction level to develop more precise pricing models."

According to Sujit, for many years the payment industry has wrestled with two primary constraints: the cost of storing large volumes of data and the difficulty of processing that data. For example, Vantiv has 800,000 clients and it processes between 200 and 300 million transactions every day. That's a lot of data to manage.

One of the ways payments companies like Vantiv make money is by carefully pricing their transactional services according to company size, transaction volume, complexity, and other vehicles. Another source of revenue involves selling data back to merchants in a form that allows them to analyze their customers' purchase behavior. Both activities require precise data management and analysis—and that's what Vantiv has set out to accomplish.

 To improve their pricing capabilities and create better new insights for customers, Sujit and the other members of Vantiv's Data and Analysis Insights team are exploring opportunities for visualizing and populating domain-specific objects from a Hadoop data lake. This big data environment, which utilizes a scalable distributed storage architecture, has lowered the cost of managing transaction data from more than $6,000 per terabyte to about $500 per terabyte.

"Big data has changed the dynamics of the industry and opened up new opportunities for nimble companies that can store, process, and especially analyze payment data," Sujit explains. "It used to be prohibitively expensive to store tens of billions of transactions, and very time-consuming to process it all. For example, it might take an hour and a half to process a hundred million records. With our current big data architecture it takes less than 20 seconds."

Actionable Insight, Data-Driven Results
Why do merchants need analytics? To eliminate guesswork, for one. To spot market trends, for another—as well as to gain insights into customer behavior and activate new sources of revenue by exploring the dynamics of their customer portfolios.

Every payment transaction in a merchant's card processing portfolio has a person behind it. Every time those individuals use a card to make a payment, they reveal important traits about themselves. Understanding the people, places, and events that drive these transactions can help merchants make informed decisions and identify new revenue opportunities.

Analyzing payment card and transaction data can also unlock new points of customer engagement, from improving loyalty and decreasing attrition to encouraging new account creation and influencing purchase behavior. Vantiv uses analytics to segment cardholder data to create customer groups, to identify suspicious activity, to create targeted marketing campaigns, and even to benchmark financial performance—so its customers can compare themselves to peer companies.

"Lots of people recognize the potential for payment analytics," Sujit explains. "However simply pointing people to a database that contains 100 billion transactions isn't very useful."

To create a more usable analytic environment, Vantiv first had to build a metadata layer that would allow them to sort, summarize, and aggregate all that raw data. Next they had to "anonymize" certain fields to mask sensitive entities, such as the names of specific merchants. Finally, they had to figure out how to represent this massive data set visually, so that users could intelligently mine the data elements and expose the attributes they were interested in. Sujit says they picked WebFOCUS for this task because it allows users to easily conduct what-if analyses and perform detailed pricing analytics on many different types of data.

"WebFOCUS is very effective for us," he says. "It gives us the data visualization and drill-down capabilities that we need. More importantly, it allows us to put the right degree of control around how we use, expose, and report on our data."

Portals, Dashboards, and InfoApps

To make use of all this information, Vantiv created a merchant portal that includes user-friendly dashboards, histograms, pie charts, InfoApps, and reports.

For example, one external-facing InfoApp combines data from the mainframe with transactions from the Hadoop big data lake, and then ties them together with geocentric codes to reveal insights about shopper habits and preferences. Merchants use this customer-facing application to better understand the purchasing behavior of their end-customers. Analysts can segment customers to develop more accurate pricing strategies.

"WebFOCUS is very effective for us," he says. "It gives us the data visualization and drill-down capabilities that we need. More importantly, it allows us to put the right degree of control around how we use, expose, and report on our data."

Another InfoApp, designed for internal users, allows Vantiv's accounting department to visually demonstrate how working capital assignments impact billing just by filtering the data attributes. "That's a big deal for the accounting guys," Sujit says, "because at the end of the day, you have to be able to show traceability on the data. This InfoApp allows us to do that."

Yet another InfoApp enables merchants to visualize important shopper statistics, such as the average basket size for a particular time or region. It can also reveal when transactions are brisk and where else customers shop within a particular zip code—insights that retailers can't get from their own point-of-sale data.

Sometimes called trust and transparency applications, these customer-facing InfoApps provide customers with vital information that boosts their confidence by demonstrating Vantiv's ability to meet their needs with targeted, high-value services. For example, many customers use the portal to create financial statements. Vantiv's PDF files utilize in-document analytics that allow people to visualize precisely the elements that they want to see. "We can send these dynamic statements to our customers, and they can mine their data directly," Sujit says.

Meanwhile, power users within each of Vantiv's lines of business can leverage the metadata layers to create their own custom reports. For instance, an analyst might benchmark customers of the same size and the same segment to develop regional pricing strategies.

Creating a Foundation for Effective Analytics

Vantiv's analytic environment includes a Hadoop data lake as well as a relational database that contains big data extracts. WebFOCUS can directly access the Hadoop platform, along with other back-end databases such as flat files on a mainframe system and an Oracle data warehouse that contains structured data.

However, as Nagesh Goteti, technology leader of data analytics and visualization at Vantiv, points out, getting the raw data in place is just the start. "We must look beyond the data to find aggregations," he explains. "The value comes when we can discover new insights for our customers."

So far, Nagesh and other members of the Data and Analysis Insights team have created four reporting universes, eight metadata layers, and an analytic Center of Excellence to help the business units gain proficiency with the analytic tools. They also created an analytic portal that contains individual tabs or "themes" for finance, sales and marketing, risk, and other business domains. An embedded security architecture governs who can see the data according to their roles within the organization. This architecture allows the IT team to easily control access to designated fields, files, folders, and analytic assets.

"We are transforming a traditional reporting-based organization into a modern data analytics-based organization, both inside and outside the firewall," Nagesh says. "WebFOCUS supports a spectrum of delivery methods, which allows us to extend analytics throughout the organization."

Vantiv continues to create a wide variety of analytic tools, from simple reports to sophisticated data-entry applications. Self-service InfoApps and analytical documents enable users to visually explore the data and answer a broad range of business questions. Casual business users can select fields and filter data within pre-defined InfoApps, while power users can use InfoAssist to create reports for themselves.

"The data is governed and users can select what they want to see," Nagesh notes. "They can build reports from the containers we have created for them, and cherry-pick the fields that are pertinent for each project. This self-service strategy is working well."

A Measurable Payback

According to Sujit, Vantiv saw a complete payback on these BI initiatives in about 12 months. He calculates this return based on three primary factors:
- Phasing out two legacy reporting platforms
- Generating additional revenue by re-pricing key customers
- Reducing the amount of time that IT professionals spend fulfilling custom report requests

"We have seen an upside of between $8 million and $15 million in revenue, annually, just by re-pricing our customers," Sujit states. "Our MIS needs are substantial, and now we can create dashboards and publish them at will."

Another big payback comes from Vantiv's use of In Document Analytics to streamline the delivery of financial statements to customers. "Our marketing guys took one look at the BI portal and said, 'We don't have to generate paper statements anymore!'" Sujit adds. "We have saved about $2.5 million now that we don't have to create so many of them."

From financial reporting to big data analytics, Vantiv now has one cohesive set of BI tools for all of its analytic needs. Does their big data prowess give them an edge in the extremely competitive payment technology services sector? Nagesh thinks so. "The company that holds the data and can analyze it to discern patterns wields tremendous power," he says. "Our everyday survival in this industry is dependent on analytics. Every payment company can complete basic transactions and provide basic services, but what you layer on top of those basic services is what gives you a competitive edge. In our case, we can analyze billions of transactions to provide actionable insights for our customers."

For years retailers have been analyzing their point of sale data to find answers to these same types of questions. However, until now, their data has been limited to what they can gather from their stores. Vantiv can provide access to aggregate data from thousands of retailers. This broad view enables merchants to study consumer-buying trends at a much more granular level. For example, a merchant can visualize the transaction data to select the optimal location for a new store.

Meanwhile, Vantiv can gather fundamental insights that help them build customer loyalty and retain current merchants. "We can answer basic questions, such as what makes them stay with us and what keeps them from shopping elsewhere for payment technology services," Nagesh says. "Our value-added analytic services compel them to stay."

Chapter Seventeen

Why The People in Our Use Cases Succeeded

While all case studies in this book are different and were designed to serve different purposes, there is a common thread in all the stories that identifies the critical factors for their successes.

First and foremost, the initiators of these apps understood the value of information in the process of business value creation. They all treated data and analytics as a business asset and they used it both strategically and tactically to enable fact-based decision-making, to deliver process enhancements, and to improve the customer experience. While many managers view data and analytics as the cost of doing business, these forward-looking individuals understood the transformational power of information—and they used it to the advantage of their organizations.

Second, they understood that information and analytics produces the most value only when put into the hands operational employees, partners, suppliers, and customers. While analytics is necessary to produce insights, operationalization is the only way to deliver the value of the insights. Hence, they turned those insights into informational products that we call InfoApps.

Third, they understood the need and value of deep technology to make these InfoApps work. People frequently underestimate the complexity in delivering information to decision makers, and thus, make optimistic promises or settle on hyped technologies that fail to deliver. The deep technology enables several critical capabilities directly related to the value of the InfoApp:

- Allows you to build a single app that reaches a large percentage of employees who can get operational intelligence regardless of their job title, rank, or knowledge. We call this: *Build once and service all.*

- Allows you to build a single app which people can use to have a dialogue with the data and get factual answers to a wide variety of questions. We call this *open-ended information access*. Contrast this with a report, which is a closed end. Every report contains answers to a fixed set of questions. If a new question arises, you have to go and request a new report. This creates the reporting bottleneck that we discussed in the prior chapters.

Deep technology enables scalability, access and integration of different data sources, complex security and data access rules, complex data queries, robust parameterization, and front-end customization. This complexity is obfuscated for the end user by a simple and intuitive interface.

Common Traits in Our Case Studies
We have identified six common traits that lead to the successful implementation and deployment of an InfoApp:
- Having the insight to create an InfoApp
- Selling the InfoApp idea internally in the organization
- Managing the cross-functional team creating the InfoApp
- Designing an effective user experience
- Managing the InfoApp as a product through its lifecycle
- Providing self-service to everyone

Let us look at each one of these in detail.

The Insight to Create an InfoApp
Every product starts as an idea, and so do the informational apps. Hence, it is important to note how such ideas originate. And while the press often attributes great product ideas, such as the iPhone and the iPad to some genius, it is often simpler than this. Take for example the insight that Deborah Repak, from the financial company FirstRate, had: "We are sitting on a treasure trove of information in our databases, and we asked ourselves: How can we help our clients glean insight from all of this data?" Deborah realized that there was an underutilized asset in her organization – the data. Data as an underutilized asset is an easy way to spot opportunities, but it requires the forward thinking of seeing the data as an asset first.

Once she had the insight, her mind was primed to watch for an opportunity to put it into practice. Here is how she describes her epiphany during conversations with clients: "The client explained how they have to extract data out of their current system to create complex spreadsheets, and then summarize it manually with Microsoft Excel. It was clearly a laborious way to get to the information that they were looking for." She then looked at what they did: "I was looking at their spreadsheets and I realized that they needed more than just a new set of reports. What they really needed was some type of analytic portal or application that would let them view their data from the top down—and then drill into exceptions based on whatever criteria they were looking for."

The key takeaway from Deborah's experience is that our mindset primes us to look for the problems to solve. Viewing data as an asset allows us to look for problems that can be solved with data and analytics. The conversations with the customers will reveal the actual needs, but solutions to the needs can only be conceived when you approach the conversation with the right mindset. To use an analogy, the dispatchers at many cab or limo services companies had screens tracking the location of each car, but none of them thought of using this information in the way that Uber did.

Selling the InfoApp Idea Internally

Every product idea requires investment in order to become a real product. Hence, all managers had to solicit resources and find organizational sponsors. Selling an app idea is not easy, but Jim Lollar's story provides an insight into how it can be done in an easy and intuitive way. Jim Lollar from Ford Motor Company explains how he sold the concept of the GWMS (Global Warranty Management System) by creating a clear vision of how dealerships would gain visibility into their warranty repair performance and how the comparison of their performance to their peers would positively affect their behavior—and Ford's bottom line. He did not have to do complex ROI studies, since it was easy to see how comparative benchmarking would drive improvements in performance. ROI assumptions take a long time to prepare and can be easily challenged, while simple behavioral traits are quite obvious and easy to understand. Thus, the key takeaway is that you can easily tie your app idea to behavioral changes that positively affect performance. In many cases, that justification is enough.

Managing the Cross-functional Team Creating the InfoApp

One essential ingredient for success when building informational applications is to establish a broad, cross-functional team. InfoApps are by nature a collaborative effort between business, IT, analysts, internal and external consultants, etc. It does not mean that the team is big, or that it will take a long time to develop. It means that since the app will touch customers and/or operations many people will be involved. The key to success is to quickly build a prototype and let the team members focus their discussion on the prototype. Seeing is believing. While many project managers think that product descriptions and requirements suffice, they can create confusion by leaving too much to the imagination of people who are not professional product managers.

The success of Steve Toth from Utz lies directly in building a quick prototype: "I was demonstrating the prototype to four executive vice presidents, and they all wanted to get SnackBoard into production immediately. The value of such a tool was clearly evident because it delivered capabilities that did not exist." But furthermore, the prototype changed the nature of the discussion: "The conversation evolved from WHAT was being presented to HOW to unlock the information to truly analyze the data. The excitement was evident and they naturally dove right in."

The key takeaway here is to give team members something real to interact with and build upon. People are better at improving products rather than at conceiving products.

Designing the User Experience

InfoApps are products. Just as with physical products, packaging matters. The look and feel of the app will influence the perception of the product. Does the application immediately appear intuitive and as easy to use as Expedia.com? Is it branded in a way that conveys your corporate style? Is it perceived as modern and on par with what people are used to seeing on the web and on their phones? Functionality is very important, but it does not trump appearance and usability. In fact, most people today perceive well-styled applications as easier to use than poorly styled ones. Thus, the very first impressions should be that the user is entirely self-sufficient.

As Luther Brown from nVision Global states, they designed the app to "make clients self-sufficient by adding more advanced analytical functionality, better drill-down capabilities, and a more elegant user experience." Furthermore, he states that adding visuals and maps enhances the customer experience because it facilitates the perception and interpretation of complex information: "Customers love that feature because they can map their lanes from Tokyo to Rotterdam or Tokyo to New York or wherever," Luther explains. "They can see how much activity was in a lane, how many shipments, how much money was involved, how much weight was involved, and so forth."

The key takeaway for designing InfoApps is to make the user self-sufficient by starting with the most important information and then allowing the user to navigate to any detail or get answers to additional questions right within the app. Use data visualization to make it easy to understand the information, and use your corporate design and colors to style the InfoApp to make it look as sharp and professional as your corporate website.

Managing the InfoApp Product Lifecycle

Every product has a lifecycle. Some products have shorter and others have longer lifecycles. Car models change every 10 years. Fashion changes every year. Thus, it is important to define and manage your product through its lifecycle. Many successful informational applications become victims of their own success. The stakeholders sometimes mistakenly believe that if it is working it should not be changed. Thus, as technology changes they start appearing dated and less user friendly. As the data changes over time, the app may become less relevant or incomplete. If there is one certain thing in the data and technology world, it is that the speed of change is fast. So be open to change, but be mindful to make it only when it's really needed. Many apps that are re-designed, just for the sake of being re-designed, fail because people do not like change for the sake of change only.

The key takeaway from Robert Kaufman at U.S. Bank is to develop the InfoApp fast: "We went from idea to implementation in about five months. Of all the technology projects I have been involved with in my career, this has been one of the simplest. I remember thinking, let's build this quickly and inexpensively, and then later we can develop something bigger and better." His advice is "Don't try to boil the ocean, get it done, get feedback from users, and then move on to the next one." Or as it happened in his case, you can leave it as it is if it works and meets the customer's needs. Robert tells us that "People enjoy the value it provides now just as much as they did six years ago."

Providing Self-Service to Everyone

Back in the day, self-service meant to consume static reports that have been pre-packaged by IT. Over the years, that definition has changed drastically as organizations started to realize that the success of their business does not only depends on delivering fast and accurate information directly into the hands of operational employees, but also on how diverse that information is. A measure of Organizational Intelligence is the range of information that is delivered to people. Steve Toth, from Utz Quality Foods, Inc. recognized the need to provide answers to business questions not only to the sales department, but also to manufacturing and finance groups, as well as using it to assist with executive-level decision-making. With so many departments using Snackboard InfoApp, it is only natural that the types of questions being asked are as different as the functions of employees who ask them. To solve this challenge, Steve has empowered employees with relevant information via an InfoApp where "one question leads to another question, which leads to another question, and so on. You don't always know where these questions will take you next. That's the power of this app. You don't have to sift through reports or hope a report exists to find the answers you need."

The key takeaway is that employees want to have a *dialogue* with the data because, as it happens, one answer frequently leads to another question. So, it is key to deliver information in open-ended applications that allow employees within an entire organization and across multiple departments to have a dialogue with the data.

Conclusion

We have been in the business intelligence and analytics business for the past 40 years developing deeper and deeper technology in response to customer needs. We have seen the emergence of many technologies that have disrupted our industry and we have adapted successfully to each one of them. Throughout all disruptions, we have remained single-focused on one core question – how information technology creates value for our customers. This has been the guiding principle for our investments in R&D.

What is especially exciting today is that data and analytics are disrupting every industry. Data and analytics are changing how business is done, how products are sold, how equipment is operated, and many more changes. This creates unprecedented opportunities for all BI and analytics professionals, and we at Information Builders are committed to support you and your enterprises in monetizing your data assets.

End Notes

1. Simon H.A., *Administrative Behavior* (4th expanded edition; first edition 1947). The Free Press, New York, 1997.

2. Howson, Cindi."BI Adoption Flat." BIScorecard. 2014. *www. biscorecard.com/ bi-adoption-flat*

3. Van Vleck, Tom. "The IBM 360/67 and CP/CMS." Multicians. December 15, 2010. *http://www.multicians.org/thvv/360-67.html*

4. Van Vleck, Tom. "The IBM 360/67 and CP/CMS." Multicians. December 15, 2010. *http://www.multicians.org/thvv/360-67.html*

5. "Carterfone decision." Computer Desktop Encyclopedia. 1981-2015. The Computer Language Company Inc. July 22, 2016. *http://encyclopedia2. thefreedictionary.com/Carterfone+decision*

6. Edwards, Benj. "A Brief History of Computer Displays." PCWorld. November 1, 2010. *http://www.pcworld.com/article/209224/displays/historic-monitors-slideshow. html#slide8.*

7. "The COBOL Programming Language." COBOL. University of Michigan, November 13. 1999. Web. July 25, 2016. *http://groups.engin.umd.umich.edu/CIS/course.des/ cis400/cobol/cobol.html.*

8. Jenkins, Tony. "On the Difficulty of Learning to Program." University of Leeds. 2002. *http://www.psy.gla.ac.uk/~steve/ localed/jenkins.html*

9. Acoustic modem. Digital image. Timeline of Innovation. SRI International. 2016. *https://www.sri.com/work/timeline-innovation/timeline.php?timeline=computing-digital#!&innovation=acoustic-modems.*

10. Scott, Jason. Computer terminal. Digital image. Flickr. N.p., August, 2013. Web. July 25, 2016. *https://www.flickr.com/photos/54568729@N00/9636183501.*

11. "Tymshare, Inc." Computer History Museum. *http://www. computerhistory.org/brochures/companies.php?alpha=t- z&company=com-42bc23cec3464*. Accessed May 23, 2016.

12. Howson, Cindi."BI Adoption Flat." BIScorecard. 2014. *www.biscorecard.com/bi-adoption-flat*

13. Postley, John. "How AT&T Works." HowStuffWorks.com. 2006. *http://money.howstuffworks.com/att4.htm*

14. AT&T's modem from 1958. Digital image. The Modem of Dennis Hayes and Dale Heatherington. Accessed May 9, 2016. *http://history-computer.com/ModernComputer/Basis/ modem.html*

15. "This Day in History: April 7, 1964." Computer History Museum. *http://www. computerhistory.org/tdih/April/7/*. Accessed May 26, 2016.

16. Howson, Cindi. "BI Adoption Flat." BIScorecard. 2014. *www.biscorecard.com/bi-adoption-flat*

17. Expedia.com is owned by Expedia Inc.

18. Davenport, Thomas H., and D.J. Patil. "Data Scientist: The Sexiest Job of the 21st Century." Harvard Business Review. October 2012. *https://hbr.org/2012/10/data-scientist-the- sexiest-job-of-the-21st-century/*

19. Piatetsky, Gregory. "Most Demanded Data Science and Data Mining Skills." KDnuggets. 2014. *http://www.kdnuggets. com/2014/12/data-science-skills-most-demand.html*

20. Manyika, James, and Michael Chui, Brad Brown, Jacques Bughin, Richard Dobbs, Charles Roxburgh, Angela Hung Byers. "Big Data: The Next Frontier for Innovation, Competition, and Productivity." McKinsey & Company. May 2011. *http://www.mckinsey.com/insights/business_technology/ big_data_the_next_frontier_for_innovation*

21. Press, Gil. "The Supply and Demand of Data Scientists: What the Surveys Say." Forbes. April 30, 2015. *http://www.forbes. com/sites/gilpress/2015/04/30/the-supply-and-demand-of- data-scientists-what-the-surveys-say/*

22. Ransbotham, Sam, David Kiron, and Pamela Kirk Prentice. "The Talent Dividend." MIT Sloan Management Review. April 25, 2015. *http://sloanreview.mit.edu/projects/analytics- talent-dividend/*

23. Davenport, Thomas H. "It's Already Time to Kill the 'Data Scientist' Title." Wall Street Journal. April 30, 2014. *http:// blogs.wsj.com/cio/2014/04/30/its-already-time-to-kill-the- data-scientist-title/*

24. Davenport, Thomas H., and D.J. Patil. "Data Scientist: The Sexiest Job of the 21st Century." Harvard Business Review. October 2012. *https://hbr.org/2012/10/data-scientist-the- sexiest-job-of-the-21st-century/*

25. Burgelman, Luc. "The Rise of the Citizen Data Scientist." NG DATA. November 5, 2015 *http://www.ngdata.com/the-rise-of- the-citizen-data-scientist/*

26. Taylor, Courtney. "What Is Simpson's Paradox?" About.com Education. About.com, March 3, 2015. Web. July 25, 2016. *http://statistics.about.com/od/HelpandTutorials/a/What-Is-Simpsons-Paradox.htm*

27. Tuna, Cari. "When Combined Data Reveal the Law of Averages." The Wall Street Journal. December 2, 2009. http:// www.wsj.com/articles/SB125970744553071829

28. We have extrapolated this number from the Bureau of Labor Statistics *http://data.bls.gov/projections/occupationProj*

29. Our estimates correlate closely with Kaggle's numbers. "Kaggle is the leading platform for data science competitions and claims to be world's largest community of data scientists. Kaggle reached 100,000 in July 2013, reported 110,000 in Sep 2013, 120,000 members on Oct 23, 2013, reported to have 140,000 on Feb 24, 2014. Latest numbers, from Kaggle CEO Anthony Goldbloom are: 157,142 Kaggle members, of whom 67,776 active in the last 6 months." (Piatetsky, Gregory. "Most Demanded Data Science and Data Mining Skills." KDnuggets. 2014. *http://www.kdnuggets. com/2014/12/data-science-skills-most-demand.html*

30. Large enterprises and SMEs tend to hire more analysts. Therefore the distribution of analysts is higher in those businesses than in the general labor population. Hence our estimates in the first chart.

31. Wohlsen, Marcus. "The Astronomical Math Behind UPS' New Tool to Deliver Packages Faster." Wired. June 13, 2013. *http://www.wired.com/2013/06/ups-astronomical-math/*

32. Kahneman, Daniel. *Thinking, Fast and Slow. New York: Farrar, Straus and Giroux*, 2011.

33. Liker, Jeffrey. *The Toyota Way: 14 Management Principles from the World's Greatest Manufacturer*. New York, NY: McGraw-Hill, 2004.

34. Craig Kelly provides a good discussion on the differences between Operational Reporting and BI in his blog "Business Intelligence vs Operational Reporting vs Financial Reporting" (*http://www.emerald-cube.com/2013/09/ovr/*)

35. Klein, Gary. *Seeing What Others Don't: The Remarkable Ways We Gain Insights*. New York, NY: PublicAffairs, 2013.

36. Klein, Gary. *Seeing What Others Don't: The Remarkable Ways We Gain Insights*. New York, NY: PublicAffairs, 2013.

37. "Kanban." Project Management History. 2016. *http://projectmanagementhistory. com/Kanban.html*. Accessed August 10, 2016.

38. Simon H.A., *Administrative Behavior* (4th expanded edition; first edition 1947). The Free Press, New York, 1997.

39. Laney, Douglas. "Infonomics: The Practice of Information Economics." Forbes. May 22, 2012. *http://www.forbes.com/sites/gartnergroup/2012/05/22/infonomics-the-practice-of-information-economics/#731578d73927*

40. Libert, Barry, Yoram (Jerry) Wind, and Megan Beck Fenley "What Airbnb, Uber, and Alibaba Have in Common." Harvard Business Review. November 20, 2014. *https:// hbr.org/2014/11/what-airbnb-uber-and-alibaba-have-in- common#*

41. Olson, Parmy. "Facebook Closes $19 Billion WhatsApp Deal." Forbes. October 6, 2014. *http://www.forbes.com/ sites/parmyolson/2014/10/06/facebook-closes-19-billion- whatsapp-deal/#52427889179e*

42. Twogood, Chris. "5 Essential Steps Toward Monetizing Your Data." Forbes. 2014. *http://www.forbes.com/sites/ teradata/2014/11/19/5-essential-steps-toward-monetizing- your-data/#134e217e3b85*

43. Manintveld, Bart, and Jorg Schalekamp. "Make money by buying and selling company data." Deloitte. 2014. *http:// www2.deloitte.com/nl/nl/pages/data-analytics/articles/make- money-buying-selling-company-data.html*

44. Wohlsen, Marcus. "The Astronomical Math Behind UPS' New Tool to Deliver Packages Faster." Wired. June 13, 2013. *http://www.wired.com/2013/06/ups-astronomical-math/*

45. Deutsch, Claudia H. "Wal-Mart throws its weight behind push to cut back on packaging." The New York Times. May 8, 2007. *http://www.nytimes. com/2007/05/08/business/ worldbusiness/08iht-package.5.5625153.html?_r=0*

46. "Wal-Mart Launches 5-Year Plan to Reduce Packaging." Walmart. September 22, 2006. *http://corporate.walmart. com/_news_/news-archive/2006/09/22/wal-mart-launches-5- year-plan-to-reduce-packaging*

47. Giang, Vivian. "How Charles Schwab Got His Workers To Produce More Steel." Business Insider. July 19, 2013. *http:// www.businessinsider.com/how-charles-schwab-got-his- workers-to-produce-more-steel-2013-7*

48. "Vitality Active Rewards with Apple Watch." Discovery Limited. *https://www.discovery.co.za/portal/individual/apple- watch-benefit*

49. Massar, Carol. "GE, the 124 Year Old Startup." Bloomberg Business Week. March 21, 2016. *http://www.bloomberg.com/ news/videos/2016-03-21/bloomberg-businessweek-ge-the- 124-year-old-startup*

50. Howson, Cindi. "BI Adoption Flat." BIScorecard. 2014. *www. biscorecard.com/ bi-adoption-flat*

51. "One Hundred Years of the Moving Assembly Line." *https:// corporate.ford.com/ innovation/100-years-moving-assembly- line.html*

52. "Capacity of container ships in seaborne trade from 1980 to 2015 (in million dwt)." Statista. *http://www.statista.com/ statistics/267603/capacity-of-container-ships-in-the-global- seaborne-trade/*

About the Authors

Gerald D. Cohen is president and CEO of Information Builders, a leader in business intelligence (BI), analytics, and data management solutions, and one of the largest privately held software companies in the world. Mr. Cohen co-founded Information Builders in 1975 with the mission to develop a software product that would allow non-programmers to create their own information systems. The resulting product, known as FOCUS, was the industry's first fourth-generation language.

Building on this foundation over the past 40 years, Information Builders' solutions have been used to drive competitive advantage, performance improvements, and innovation for thousands of leading companies, universities, healthcare providers, and government agencies around the world.

Dr. Rado Kotorov, Ph.D., is a visionary, innovator, and strategist with many years of experience in the BI and analytics industry. During his tenure at Information Builders, he has been instrumental in the release of key products such as Active Technologies, InfoAssist, Magnify, RStat, Enable, and others. He and Gerald Cohen co-invented and hold a patent for the underlying technology in Active Technologies. Dr. Kotorov has a Ph.D. in Decision and Game Theory and Economics from Bowling Green State University.